# BUILDING UP
## 6 SIMPLE SPIRITUAL DISCIPLINES FOR STUDENTS

# ETHAN SMITH

College&Clayton Press
ATHENS, GEORGIA

# College&Clayton
## Press

College and Clayton Press website: https://collegeandclayton.com

Cover and Interior Design: Daniel Blake Hulsey

ISBN: 978-1-956553-19-2

Set the believers an example.

1 Timothy 4:12

Therefore, as you received Christ Jesus the Lord, so walk in him, rooted and built up in him and established in the faith, just as you were taught, abounding in thanksgiving.

Colossians 2:6-7,

Rather train yourself for godliness; for while bodily training is of some value, godliness is of value in every way, as it holds promise for the present life and also for the life to come. The saying is trustworthy and deserving of full acceptance. For to this end we toil and strive, because we have our hope set on the living God,

1 Timothy 4:7-10

God gave the growth.

1 Corinthians 3:6

# CONTENTS

# ACKNOWLEDGMENTS

There are so many people who influence any given book. This being my first book, the list is incredibly long. I am thankful to my pastor, Daniel Palmer, for suggesting this book should be written, and that I should be the one to do it. Not only did he give the idea, but he took the time to look over every word. His careful eye not only helped for any sentence, but also helped to clarify my own thinking. I am grateful for your friendship, and the church we get to serve, North Roanoke Baptist Church. However hard he worked to straighten it out, every mistake remains completely my own.

To College and Clayton publishing, thank you for taking a risk on a young man with an idea and a desire to be helpful to the rising generation of Christians. I so appreciate your work, and I look forward to seeing what the Lord does through you.

My family has taught me so much over the years, often more by showing than by telling. Seeing Bible reading, serving, and giving built in me these habits long before any college course or book taught me their value. I am so grateful to the Lord for giving me a family who so loved God, the church, and me. It is a blessing I see far more clearly now than I ever did growing up.

Even now, as a husband and parent, I carry those lessons and examples my father and grandfather lived out in front of me. I still cherish the opportunity to have conversations with my grandfather about what the Lord is teaching and showing us in His Word. They mean more to me than you will ever know.

To my wife who, apart from the salvation found in Christ, is God's greatest blessing to me; I am so thankful for your love and encouragement. No part of my life or ministry would be possible without you. Thank you isn't enough. I am so grateful to the Lord for putting us together.

To my beautiful girls, Charlotte and Olivia, I hope you will grow up to love the Lord Jesus Christ far more than you will love anything else, including your mom and me. I pray for this every night. I hope the disciplines found in this book will become a part of your life early on, and the Lord will use you for amazing things. You bring more joy to your father's heart than you will ever know. Daddy loves you!

# FOREWORD

The Christian life is built on essentials. There are foundational truths that are non-negotiable and define our faith. There are core doctrines and convictions that anchor our beliefs. Beliefs like "Jesus is fully human and fully God." or "God is Triune." In addition to these timeless truths, there are indispensable disciplines that are vital building blocks as well. These spiritual habits promote our spiritual growth as we trust and follow Jesus. Similar to a sport that requires running, dribbling, throwing, or passing, without these fundamental practices we simply can't be successful in our Christian walk!

These spiritual disciplines are essential for several reasons. First and foremost, it's because they help us enter and encounter God's presence. They foster a deeper personal relationship with Christ through communion with him. He speaks to us through his word and shapes our hearts through prayer. And as we worship, serve, give, and share our faith, his Spirit within us resonates with his work around us. The spiritual disciplines are the opportunities for personal interaction and fellowship with our Savior that give us life. In this sense, they're essential like breathing.

The spiritual disciplines are also necessary because they nurture our spiritual health. The disciplines help us grow. They provide spiritual nourishment for our souls while helping us remove the harmful contaminants in our hearts. In other words, they cultivate godly desires and eliminate sinful desires. They empower us for God's work and strengthen us to overcome the trials, troubles, and temptations of the world. Without the spiritual disciplines, we are weak, ill-equipped, and spiritually malnourished. In this sense, they're essential like eating.

Finally, spiritual disciplines are vital because they humble us and train us to submit to God. Since these devotional habits are commanded, practicing them is a matter of obedience. Not as routines, rituals, or religious performance, but in submission to God. They ultimately condition our hearts to learn, obey, trust, and follow him in full surrender. Apart from physical activity, our muscles atrophy and we can't perform even the most basic functions. In this sense, spiritual disciplines are essential like exercise.

Sadly, too many times in the church, and especially in student ministry, we challenge God's people to be devoted to these essential disciplines without actually equipping them to follow through and practice them. We not only fail to provide the instructions and explain the 'how,' we often neglect the biblical rationale that answers the 'why.' But in *Building Up*, Ethan Smith provides a helpful resource to help us overcome this glaring oversight in student ministry. It's both, insightful and useful. It will not only help explain 'why' the disciplines are essential, it will equip you with the 'how' to make them practical.

I pray that this book will be a helpful resource that God uses in your life as you "grow in the grace and knowledge of our Lord and Savior Jesus Christ" (2 Pet 3:18). In the spirit of the apostle Paul's challenge to the Colossians, "As you received Christ Jesus the Lord, so walk in him, rooted and built up in him and established in the faith, just as you were taught, abounding in thanksgiving" (Col 2:6-7).

In His grace,
R. Scott Pace

# Introduction:
## Is It Worth It?

Spiritual disciplines. I am willing to bet this topic is not high on your priority list. After all, you are busy with school, friends, sports, or other important tasks. Why would you take the time to read a short book about living the Christian life? Maybe this is the first time you have even heard of the phrase "spiritual disciplines."

My guess is you are a student that is looking for some help on how to grow in your life as a Christian. I am not that old (28 at the time of writing this particular sentence), but I can remember being a Christian and wondering, 'what in the world am I supposed to do?' I was told to read my Bible, pray, and tell my friends about Jesus, but I was often left wondering 'how in the world am I supposed to do that?' I was never really given any guidance. It was frustrating.

It was like I was told it was my job to build a bridge across a river. Everyone who joined the team all had to build the bridge. We all knew we had to build it, and everyone expected the others to do it, but not many of us actually knew what to do. We were never given any schematics or blueprints. They pointed to a bunch of boards and nails and told me to get to work. Shockingly, I was left a bit frustrated.

The goal of this book is to help students build the bridge. I want to help them like I wish I was helped.

The idea for this book originated in a conversation with my pastor about books I could give to the students in our student ministry (I am the student pastor at my church). I have been helped so much by reading, and I want to help my students by introducing them to a few good books. I know I am a nerd. You don't need to tell me that.

My pastor mentioned it would be helpful for students to have a book to explain some of the practical disciplines of the Christian life in a student-friendly way. Spiritual disciplines are tasks done by Christians sometimes daily, weekly, or monthly that help stir our love for Jesus and help us live faithfully for Him. They are called *disciplines* because they do take effort. You might find that some come more naturally than others. However, as a follower of Christ, we need to work on growing in all the areas, not just the ones that come easily. This is why discipline is necessary.

They are also *spiritual*. This means the focus is on God, not on the stuff around us. You might be disciplined enough to get up and practice basketball every morning before most of us are even out of bed. That is a discipline that focuses on this life, and specifically how good you are at a particular sport. It is crucial if you are going to improve your skill as a player, but the focus is basketball.

The focus of spiritual disciplines is to get our eyes off of ourselves and put them on our Triune God. We will only grow as Christians when we focus on Him. This is a lesson I wish I heard at an earlier age. The goal is never to simply finish a checklist, like the to-do list you are given to clean the house. The goal is to know God in a deeper way, to love Him, find our joy in Him, and to live in obedience to Him for our entire lives. It is a relationship more than tasks. It is a marathon, not a sprint. It will take time and effort. It is a lifelong process. We need to get started.

The most important question for you to ask and answer before you read another page is this: Is Jesus worth it? How you answer this question will largely determine whether or not you are willing to put in the effort these disciplines require to grow as a Christian. It is a question we cannot avoid.

This makes sense in other areas of our lives, right? Being good at basketball is worth the time and effort of getting up early to work out and practice. Playing the piano well is worth the hours of practice involved. Performing your part in the theatre production is worth the time spent learning lines and rehearsing. If these goals weren't worth it, then you wouldn't put in the time and effort. It is pretty simple. You want to improve, so you train.

Is Jesus worth it? Have you ever thought of it like this? Is reading your Bible or going to church just something you do because you know you are supposed to? That may work for a little while, but it will not be enough when life gets hard or busy. What happens on the first Sunday of your college career, when your parents aren't waking you up to go to church? What do you do? Is it still worth it?

I want you to read this loud and clear: Jesus is worth it. He came to bring life and life abundantly (Jn. 10:10). He took on the wrath of God we owed as sinners, even though He was sinless, so we could be brought back to God in this life and spend eternity with Him. He is the Treasure that will satisfy your soul. He is the One for whom you were made. He is better than good grades. He is better than sports, even being a professional athlete. He is better than relationships. He is better because He will never leave you or abandon you. He died in your place to free you from sin. He is more than worth anything this world has to offer.

It is in Him that we find joy, joy that goes deeper than a sunny day and our favorite meal. In Him is life. In His presence is the fullness of joy. At His right hand are pleasures forevermore (Ps. 16:11). This is what I want for every single one of you. I want you to know the love of God that surpasses understanding. That was

Paul's prayer for the Ephesians, and it is my prayer for you (Eph. 3:14-19).

Living as a Christian is hard. I don't want to pretend like it is easy. The message of the Bible is not if we follow Jesus then everything is going to go exactly like we want. Indeed, Jesus tells us we will face difficulties, but we can have confidence because He has overcome them (Jn. 16:33). He is the goal of the Christian life. The amazing reality of the Christian life is we get God!

So, from the beginning of this book, you need to decide if Jesus is worth it. Is He worth the struggle? The answer of the Bible, and from my own experience (which is far less important than the Bible), is yes, He is. Following Christ faithfully is worth any and every effort and difficulty you might face. He is better than you can even begin to imagine. You were made to know and love God and, as Augustine says, our hearts will be restless until they rest in Him.

Do you believe it? Do you really believe Jesus is as glorious as the Bible tells us He is? Do you believe He is worth any effort to have more of Him? I pray so. It will not be easy. Spiritual disciplines take time to develop; but they are worth it. I hope that this book will be helpful in forming habits of discipline that will bring you more joy in Christ that will last both now and into eternity.

# Chapter 1:
# Bible Intake: Why?

You need to read your Bible. I have heard that a lot over my time in church. Well-meaning Sunday School teachers or my youth leaders were quick to tell me how important it was for me to read the Bible. They were right! After all, everything we do in church centers around this one Book (or at least it should). However, what I often didn't hear was how or why.

I don't blame them. They were doing exactly what I am doing in this book. I want you to read your Bible. It is really important if you are going to grow as a Christian for you to spend time reading your Bible, but I don't want to leave you hanging on *why* we should take the time to read it.

Many of us, though, just don't like to read. I was like that until around college. However, the fact that you are holding this book in your hand right now tells me that you are at least interested in reading the Bible more consistently. That alone is a huge first step. You just might need a little encouragement.

I have found reading in general, and reading the Bible specifically, is appetitive. This means the more you try something, the more you find that you like it. Take something like drinking coffee as an example. Not many people drink coffee for the first time and fall in love with the taste. It is too bitter. It is too strong. I would prefer sweet tea (I was raised on sweet tea, so it is my standard for all other drinks).

However, the more you try it, the more you might find yourself liking it. At first, it is gross; then it is not so bad; then you find

yourself ordering a drink at Starbucks that you can barely pro-
nounce, but you know you love it. It takes time. Your taste for it
develops the more you try. Although, the coffee I drink every
morning has enough sugar and creamer in it to basically negate
the coffee taste. I am still working on it. It is far better than it
used to be.

It can be the same with reading the Bible. The more you do it, the
more you will find that you enjoy reading it. It may not happen
overnight, and that is okay. Things worth doing rarely are easy.
Sometimes, though, we need to be reminded why the Bible is so
important for us as Christians. Reading your Bible is not a discipline that you grin and bear, like eating your Brussel sprouts as a
kid. It is one that God graciously allows us to enjoy. It is more like
honey, and less like the little cabbages. David says the law of the
God is "more to be desired than gold" and "sweeter also than
honey" (Ps. 19:10). It is valuable and it is sweet. We get to enjoy it.
It can become a pleasure to us.

Let's talk about what the Bible is, why we should believe it, and
why we need it to grow as a Christian. This will help us understand how precious it is and enable us to enjoy it a little more.

## JESUS'S VIEW OF THE BIBLE

A few years ago, a popular bracelet was seen on the arms of every
cool Christian guy and girl. You could not go to a summer camp
or student conference without seeing them. Most students
would buy their own. I actually still have one. I am talking about
the WWJD bracelets.

These colorful bracelets were seen everywhere. They were meant
to remind the wearer to think about Jesus outside of the church
walls. The bracelets helped us to always ask the question, "What
would Jesus do?" Whenever we faced a problem, we were told to
ask what Jesus would do if He were in the same situation.
Although the bracelets became a little cliché, the question that is

being posed on the bracelet is valuable. We should think about what Jesus would do when we are facing a difficult situation. Here's the problem: the bracelets leave *us* to answer the question.

To answer that question accurately, however, we must go to the Bible to see what He actually tells us to do; and I don't just mean the red-lettered words. The entire Bible is God's Word to us. All sixty-six books of the Old and New Testament.

Hold on for a second. That is a loaded statement we cannot let slide by without stopping to think about it. All sixty-six books of the Old and New Testament are the Word of the living God. Since God is the God of truth, every word of the Bible is also true (Heb. 6:18; Jn. 14:6; 16:13). However, I don't want you just to take my word for it. Instead, we should ask the question 'what did Jesus believe?' How did He view the Bible?

After all, if Jesus is the Son of God, then He is omniscient (He knows everything). If He knows everything, then He knows what is right and true. Therefore, whatever His view is on any subject is correct. He cannot be wrong and still be the "Truth" (Jn. 14:6).[1] We can trust Him to tell us what is right. This is why we should investigate what Jesus believes in order to help us in our own belief. The four Gospels are a helpful place to begin.

There are numerous examples in the Gospels of Jesus quoting Scripture. He does so when He is being tempted by Satan in the wilderness (Mt. 4:1-11; Lk. 4:1-13). In doing so, He shows the authority of Scripture. When going toe-to-toe with the prince of darkness, the weapon Jesus used was the sword of the Spirit, which is the Word of God (Eph. 6:17). He trusted that what was written in the Old Testament carried with it the authority of God, much like the badge of a police officer carries the authority of the state. In that moment, to the Bible Jesus went. Why wouldn't we do the same when we are tempted?

He knew it was right. He knew it would stand any test from Satan. It was His defense. If He thought it was lacking or needed improvement, then He would not have turned to it at His moment of need. He knew it would not let Him down.

Another example is found in John 10. First, we need to set the scene. Jesus is teaching and has just declared one of the most magnificent realities in all of the Bible, that He is the Good Shepherd who lays down His life for His sheep. Of course, Jesus is not speaking about actual sheep. He is using sheep as a metaphor for His people. He is the Shepherd of His people who loves them, protects them, cares for them, and lays down His life for their salvation.

Even more counterculture, these sheep are not just from the fold of the Jews, which would have been surprising to His listeners. He has other sheep that are not of that fold, and He will bring them in also (Jn. 10:16). He is saving people from every nation, tribe, people, and languages (Rev. 7:9). Redemption is for sinners all over the world! I am writing this in Roanoke, Virginia, a long way from Israel. I have no Jewish roots. This promise that He will save others outside of the Jews is why I am here. Praise the Lord!

Even though I am excited and thankful for these words of Jesus, not everyone was at the time. The Jews begin to surround Jesus and question Him for His teaching, with the end result that they pick up stones to kill Him. Things are escalating rather quickly. It went from a conversation to a mob ready to kill. This won't be the last time a scene shifts like this for Jesus.

Jesus sees the situation and asks them a valid question. He says, "I have shown you many good works from the Father; for which of them are you going to stone me?" (Jn. 10:32). This seems reasonable, right? Jesus has performed many good works for all to see. Why would they want to stone Him? Why exactly are they so mad at Him?

They reply, "It is not for a good work that we are going to stone you but for blasphemy, because you, being a man, make yourself God" (v. 33). Blasphemy is speaking against God or, in this case, saying that you are God. This is an offense that warrants the death penalty in Hebrew law. It is a serious accusation. Is He doing this? Yes, He is. Jesus has already said that He and the Father are one (v. 30). Jesus has declared for all to hear that God is His Father and that they are one. This is a blasphemous statement coming from the lips of a man. Unless, it is true. Here is the rub. This was the problem with the Jewish leaders. They could not believe this man could really be who He claimed to be, namely the Son of God.

Hang with me, we are getting to the connection to the Bible.

The scene continues, "Jesus answered them, "Is it not written in your Law, 'I said, you are gods'? If he called them gods to whom the word of God came—and Scripture cannot be broken—do you say of him whom the Father consecrated and sent into the world, 'You are blaspheming,' because I said, 'I am the Son of God'?" (vs. 34-36).

Jesus answers their accusation by quoting a seemingly obscure Psalm back to them. If Psalm 82:6 calls these individuals 'gods' (notice with the lower case 'g'), then why would they be upset when He calls Himself the Son of God. If earthly princes can be called gods, then why cannot the true Son of God call Himself God? After all, the Scripture cannot be broken. If the religious leaders believe the Bible, then they have no reason to be mad. Either they believe it, or they don't. They cannot want the Bible when it helps their case and discard it when it doesn't. They cannot have it both ways. Jesus will not let this pass. They don't have a reply, or don't want to offer one, and He slips away from the confrontation.

What we need to notice is the little aside that is almost a throwaway line. There are no accidental words or statements in the

Bible. Every word is there for a reason. The Scripture cannot be broken. This is our Lord's view of the Bible. It cannot be broken.

I never attended karate as a kid. It was not something remotely on my radar. If you were to hand me a block of wood and ask me to break it without any tools, then I would tell you that it cannot be broken. I don't want to break my hand trying, nor do I want you to laugh at me when I scream in pain as my hand hits the wood. It would not be a pretty scene. I am not going to do it.

However, if you were to take that same block of wood to a black belt in karate, then the wood becomes far more breakable. We can both watch in amazement as this individual, perhaps with ease, punches through the wood. What would have broken my hand and made you laugh would have splintered as this master performs the task. Instead of laughing and crying, we would be applauding.

Scripture is not like the block of wood. It cannot be broken. There are no 'masters' who can undo what God has already done. There is no way to shatter what God has brought together. The Book you hold in your hands is the Word of God. It cannot be broken. Your Savior and Lord believes it. So should we.

We can trust the Bible. It will not crumble under the weight of your situation, your problem, or the culture around you. There are no scientific discoveries or archeological finds that will truly discredit the Bible when properly understood. You can have confidence in the Bible because it is unbreakable. Jesus says so.

## THE SUFFICIENCY OF SCRIPTURE.

"This is great," you might be thinking, "but how does that help me in my actual problems?" Sure, it is cool that Jesus believed the Bible is the Word of God and cannot be broken, but that doesn't mean it is going to help me now. If we are being honest, we often pick up the Bible and are hoping to find direct answers to our questions, rather than opening the Bible in order to see Jesus. This is why we are often left frustrated. It is not meant to be a how-to manual, but a window through which we see God, and the world, rightly. It provides help in every situation, but not often in the way we think. This is why we need discipline, because sometimes those answers are not easily found.

What we must believe, as a foundation, is that God has given us exactly what we need to live the Christian life. He has not saved us and then given us a Where's Waldo book. If you remember these books from your favorite doctor's or dentist's office, then you know the two pages are full of pictures, usually of a massive scene, like a beach or a zoo. Your job in all of the chaos is to find Waldo. He is always dressed in the same red and white striped shirt and hat. You would think he would be easy to spot, but I have been called back for my teeth cleaning many times before I found the expert of hiding in plain sight.

God is not like this. He has not given us a book that was meant to trick us and hide what we need. We will readily admit that there are some things in the Bible that are mysterious and hard to understand. Peter admits this about Paul's writing (2 Pet. 3:15-16). This should make us feel better when we don't understand something in the Bible, at least it does for me. If Peter, who walked with Jesus for three years, did not understand everything that Paul was writing, then it is okay if we don't either. Yet, God, as a loving Father, has given us what we need in order to grow as a Christian in every area of our lives.

Don't take my word for it though. Second Timothy 3:16-17 says, "All Scripture is breathed out by God and profitable for teaching, for reproof, for correction, and for training in righteousness, that the man of God may be complete, equipped for every good work." It might helpful if we break these verses down a little.

"All Scripture." That seems like a pretty obvious statement for Christians. We know what "All Scripture" means in this verse, right? Before we jump to any conclusions, we need to take a look at the context around our verse.

In verses 14-15, Timothy is told to continue in what he has been taught and believed since his childhood. Timothy had been blessed, like many of us, with relatives who taught him the Bible. Paul says he has been acquainted with the "sacred writings, which are able to make you wise for salvation through faith in Christ Jesus" (v. 15). If you have grown up in a family who has taught you the Bible, be thankful to God. Not everyone enjoys this blessing, and there are many who wish they had your experience.

Paul tells Timothy to continue in what he has believed since childhood. He had been taught well and shouldn't try to progress past what he had been taught. We can pick up a lot of different beliefs from our parents, some good, some bad, and some indifferent. The sports teams I follow now as an adult have largely been dictated by who my parents cheered for when I was growing up. I am a Boston Celtics fan today because my dad started following the Celtics in the 80's. One reason I developed the habit of reading my Bible daily is because I saw my parents read their Bible's before they went to bed. I am thankful to God for this blessing in my childhood.

If you didn't grow up with this type of example, then hear me my plea: be the example for the next person. Make a commitment to the Bible so that your friends around you, your church, and your future children will be acquainted with the Bible through you. You can develop this habit right now. I pray you do.

These "sacred writings" are the Scripture that is being referred to in verse 16. What is the Scripture? It is, what we now call, the Old Testament. This is what Timothy would have known as Scripture. This makes sense because the New Testament had not been completed. After all, the Second Letter to Timothy is contained in the New Testament.

It is important to notice that these sacred writings are writings that will lead one to salvation through faith in Jesus Christ. Paul believes that if one is familiar with the Old Testament, he is in great position to receive Christ through faith. If we read the Old Testament well, it leads us to Jesus. This should not be a surprise. Didn't Jesus tell the religious leaders, "You search the Scriptures because you think that in them you have eternal life; and it is they that bear witness about me" (Jn. 5:39)? Paul writes, "Christ is the end of the law for righteousness to everyone who believes" (Rom. 10:4). Christ is the end goal of the law. It points to Him.

However, it isn't wrong that our minds immediately go to the entire sixty-six books of the Bible when we see the phrase "all Scripture." There are solid, biblical reasons for believing the New Testament is included as a part of "all Scripture." I will give you a few of these reasons.

The first reason is that Jesus tells His disciples that the Holy Spirit will continue to teach them after Jesus has departed. He says, "I still have many things to say to you, but you cannot bear them now. When the Spirit of truth comes, he will guide you into all the truth, for he will not speak on his own authority, but whatever he hears he will speak, and he will declare to you the things that are to come. He will glorify me, for he will take what is mine and declare it to you" (Jn. 16:12-14).

Did you catch what Jesus was saying in this passage? He is not done teaching the disciples, even though He is about to go to the cross the next day. How is He going to continue to teach them, and, by extension, us two thousand years later? The answer is the Holy Spirit. The Holy Spirit is going to come and guide the disciples into all truth. This truth will then be recorded in the pages of Scripture and carry with it the authority of Jesus. After all, it is His Word to them, and us. This is why we consider the product of this guidance, namely the twenty-seven books of the New Testament, to be on the same level as the Old Testament, God's Word to us.

This might make me sound terrible, but I actually enjoy it when a professional athlete makes a mistake. That might sound bad, but come on. It is easy to laugh when an NBA star misses a dunk, or an NFL running back falls down mid-play. It makes me feel better about myself to know that they are not perfect either. Does that make me a horrible person? I don't think so.

When I am reading the Bible and one of the disciples is confused or doubts, then it makes me feel a little better about my own struggles to understand. I believe these instances are in the Bible so that we remember that there is only one perfect Person, and that is Jesus. Everyone else is a sinner, me included. One text that encourages me is 2 Peter 3:15-16. It says, "And count the patience of our Lord as salvation, just as our beloved brother Paul also wrote to you according to the wisdom given him, as he does in all his letters when he speaks in them of these matters. There are some things in them that are hard to understand, which the ignorant and unstable twist to their own destruction, as they do the other Scriptures."

What is so encouraging about this text is Peter says that there are some things that are hard to understand in Paul's letters. That makes me feel better. When I read Paul's letters there are moments where I encounter something that is difficult, and you will too. It is nice to know that even the Apostle Peter felt the same way.

Take heart when you read and study the Bible. You will not understand everything on your first read. Meaning may come only after a lot of thought, effort, time, and frustration. This is never an excuse to stop. It is actually all the more reason to continue. If we want to dig a well, we must keep digging until we find water. The water is present. We need to keep working. I just want you to know from the beginning, it will not always be easy. In fact, count on it being hard.

Isn't that the lesson we hear from our parents, teachers, and coaches though? Anything worth doing comes with difficulty. You can bet your favorite musician didn't become great because he quit when his hands started hurting; or Stephen Curry didn't quit playing basketball because he missed a lot when he was growing up; or your favorite actress didn't leave Hollywood because she wasn't offered the role she wanted the moment she arrived. No. The ones we admire and follow were committed to their craft even when it became difficult. How much more should we be willing to put forth whatever effort is necessary when our prize is Jesus? Our Treasure is far greater. We need to realize it, believe it, and live like it.

The Bible that you hold in your hand, all sixty-six books, are the Scripture. The entire Bible is God's Word to us. Paul says this Scripture is 'God-breathed'. I like the ESV translation here, but your translation may say that Scripture is 'inspired by God'. That can be a little misleading because 'inspiration' doesn't mean for us today what it means in this passage.

Artists are inspired to paint a beautiful picture. They may wait weeks for inspiration to strike. You may be inspired by a book or movie. These are good feelings that encourage us onward. The hero showed courage, and so should we. This is the inspiration we often feel. This is not what takes place in the Bible. Paul doesn't just sense God being near and write about it. Isaiah doesn't have goosebumps after an awesome worship song, so he writes about the judgment.

What the text means by "breathed out by God" goes deeper than this. Paul means that the very words of the Bible were given by God. The theological designation that is used is: verbal plenary inspiration. This sounds difficult, but it is actually pretty simple.

Verbal means words. God inspired the actual words that are used in the Scripture. He didn't inspire just the authors who then wrote whatever they wanted. No. God inspired the words themselves. Plenary means full, complete, entire.[2] If we put these two together, then we understand what is being conveyed. All the words of the Bible were fully given by God through the human authors. Or, as J. I. Packer notes, "What Scripture says, God says."[3]

When Paul says that all of Scripture is breathed out by God, he means the entirety of Scripture is given by God and is, therefore, authoritative and inerrant. Simply put, the Bible carries the authority of God and is without error. This is why we trust the Bible and obey the Bible.

Authority is important. We are supposed to listen to people with authority. In almost every teen show ever (I have no data to back up this claim, just my own observation) there is a scene in which the teenager gets into an argument with his parents because he wants to do something that his parents have told him not to. The line that usually comes from the parents is something like, "As long as you live under my roof you will live by my rules." Sound familiar? We are meant to feel how unfair this is. Authority is so restricting and mean, right?

Nope. Authority is actually a good thing. It is meant to protect us. It is meant to help us flourish when used rightly. We have an obligation to obey those in authority. We don't always like it, but we still must. Because God is the Creator of everything, He has authority over it all. He gets to call the shots and make the rules. The wonderful reality is that His rules are not random. He is good (1 Chr. 16:34). He is righteous (Ps. 11:7). We can trust that He will do what is right (Gen. 18:25).

The character of God should amplify our desire to obey Him. Since He is good and wants the best for us, and has provided the best in Christ (Rom. 8:32), wouldn't it be in our best interest to listen to Him? Since He is omniscient, wouldn't He know better than we how life should be lived? After all, He is the One who designed it in the first place. It seems reasonable to listen to the

One who loves us, made us, and created the world around us. The Bible on your desk or by your bed carries with it authority that is not based on you, your parents, or your pastor. The authority comes from God. Therefore, our job is to read it, believe it, and obey it.

Since the words are God-breathed, they must be true. God cannot lie (Num. 23:19; Tit. 1:2). Since He cannot lie, everything He says can be trusted. Since Scripture is His Word, we can trust that the Bible is completely true. God will never lie to you. He will not deceive you or try to trick you. He will always tell the truth, and He has in His Word.

You may be asking, "What does that have to do with reading the Bible?" All of this is not superfluous. It is crucial if we are going to understand the heart of Paul's statement in 2 Timothy 3:16-17. As we shift to how the Scripture is to be applied, we need to first understand and believe that God is the Author, the Scripture has authority, and Scripture is true. If we don't understand the reasoning behind it, then we will be quick to set the Bible aside when it tells us something that we don't like. Trust me, you will find things in the Bible that are not immediately pleasant to you. This is why we need to believe God and trust that He knows what He is doing. His way is always the best.

## Sufficient for the Christian Life

One question that you might be thinking after reading all of this is: "so what? Does this actually mean anything for my walk with Jesus? Will this help with my day-to-day life?" Let me assure you. Yes, the Bible is the most practical book you will read. The Bible contains everything you need to follow Christ for your entire life. If you had no other Christian books, but only the Bible, then you would be just fine.

Let's look back at 2 Timothy 3:16-17. Paul writes, "All Scripture is breathed out by God and profitable for teaching, for reproof, for correction, and for training in righteousness, that the man of God may be complete, equipped for every good work."

Profitable means beneficial. Scripture is helpful for us. It is worth the time and effort. Why are you willing to get up early in order to work out? It is because it will be profitable when the football season starts. Why are you spending so much time studying for your test that is coming up next week? It is because it will allow you to do well on your test. Why do you go to work? It is beneficial for you. You get paid real money to go to work. At first you may not like doing any of these tasks, but you find you come to enjoy them because you see the benefit.

Reading and studying the God-breathed Bible is more like building a house than it is building a pillow fort when you were a kid. When you were a kid and it was a rainy day, it was so much fun to build a pillow fort. You get all the blankets together and make a structure. You stacked them up just right and covered them with the blankets. Maybe you watch a movie under your fort and hang out with your friends (who could only enter by saying the right password). It was enjoyable for the afternoon, but then it came time to clean up. The structure you built was just as easily torn down.

Building a brick house is different. It takes time and effort. You accomplish it one brick at a time. You might work all day and not see much result. It might not look like you are making much of a difference. After a while though, you can look back and see how far you have come. The house is beginning to take shape. The work is worth it. So it is with reading the Bible and taking it into our lives. We know it is good for us and will help us live the Christian life, even when we don't see immediate results. We build the house of our Christian life one Bible reading at time. It is worth it. If God tells us it is profitable, then we know it is.

It is profitable in several ways. It is profitable for teaching. We learn more about God and His Son as we read and study the Bible. If He is our Treasure, then gaining more of this treasure is always worth it. Your greatest need is to know God. Therefore, to know Him in His Word is the biggest reward you could possibly want. He is an inexhaustible fountain of joy and life. You will always find more in Him to see and enjoy. However, learning is not enough if it doesn't translate into our actions. When it doesn't, we must be reproved.

This is a full turnaround. It is a hard stop. When you are reading the Bible then you will inevitably come across sins in your life that you need to stop outright. An example is Colossians 3:5, which says, "Put to death therefore what is earthly in you: sexual immorality, impurity, passion, evil desire, and covetousness, which is idolatry." This is an outright command. We are to put to death what is earthly in us, such as sexual immorality. It cannot be tolerated. It must be killed. That means a struggle with pornography is not a small sin that we live with. It needs to be killed. Harsh language to show how serious this is. This is walking down one path, stopping, and going to opposite direction. Scripture will reprove you. Praise the Lord, this is a wonderful reality. We need it.

It will also correct us. If you have ever ridden on an airplane, then you understand how important course precision is. If you are slightly off course at the beginning of the flight, by the end you could be hundreds of miles from where you wanted to go. It is easier to correct the flight path at the beginning than it is to do a major shift at the end. You don't want a massive layover in a different city because your pilot was slightly off course.

Take something like attending church. Hebrews 10:25 commands us not to neglect meeting together. We need to be with other Christians in worship if we are going to continue on in faithfulness to Christ. This is not to say it is always wrong to miss church. If you are sick, it is probably better to take a week off than risk getting others sick. However, when the next week rolls around and you are feeling better, then comes the moment of truth. Are you going to return to church or not? Correction can say, "the Bible tells me that I need to worship Christ with other believers", even though I enjoyed watching online last week, I need to get back to church. We correct the course slightly, so we don't need to be reproved later.

"And for training in righteousness, that the man of God may be complete, equipped for every good work." We are to be holy because God is holy (1 Pet. 1:15-16). God cares about how we live. We are His representatives in the world. We are His ambassadors (2 Cor. 5:20). Just as He is holy, we are to be holy. We are to be righteous. This isn't natural for us because "no one is righteous, no, not one" (Rom. 3:10). We have our righteousness from Jesus (2 Cor. 5:21). This is our right standing before God. What about our actions though? We must be trained. But how?

God has given us His Word to train us to live in obedience to Him. Everything we need to live the Christian life is found in the Bible. How do I know? It is because through Scripture we are made "complete, equipped for every good work." Every single good work that God has created us to accomplish (Eph. 2:10), He has equipped us to do through His Word. He hasn't forgotten to tell us something we need. It is all there. Our job is to take up and read.

There is nothing worse than being expected to perform when you haven't been trained. It is so discouraging. I think about being in school and the teacher is out for a week and the substitute doesn't actually teach anything. Sure, it is a lot of fun in the moment. We watch movies and do nothing. But when the teacher gets back and gives a test on what we should have learned, then the fun is over. It is not fair because the substitute didn't teach the class, and now they are going to fail as a result. Not a great feeling. We would feel like we are being cheated.

God is not like that. He is not going to call you to do something that He first hasn't already done in Christ. Keep in mind, Jesus lived a sinless life (Heb. 4:15), which means He actually knows what it is like to be tempted and not give in. However, God doesn't just give us an example to follow, He gives us instructions on how to live. Everything we need is found in the Bible. Not only has He given us His Word to train, but also His Spirit to empower (Phil. 2:13; Col. 1:29). As John Piper puts it, "everything you need in order to be saved, to live a life of faith that pleases God, and to persevere to the end, [God has] declared to you."[4] For that, we should be thankful. We will not be able to stand before God on judgment day and say we were never told. We don't have that excuse.

Take heart. The Bible is worth the effort. It is worth the commitment. It is worth the time. In the next chapter, we will move on to the practical aspects of Bible intake. However, if you don't see why it is important, the how won't matter as much. It is my prayer that this is helping you love Jesus and see the importance of His Word, and how precious of a gift it is to have a God-breathed book.

# Chapter Endnotes

[1] Credit goes to the late R. C. Sproul for introducing this line of thinking to me.

[2] "Plenary Definition & Meaning," Dictionary.com (Dictionary.com), accessed September 21, 2022, https://www.dictionary.com/browse/plenary.

[3] J. I. Packer, *Concise Theology* (Wheaton, IL: Crossway, 2020), 23.

[4] John Piper, *Providence* (Wheaton, IL: Crossway, 2020), 610.

# CHAPTER 2:
# BIBLE INTAKE: HOW?

Now that we have successfully covered why you should read your Bible, we can talk about how to develop the habit. This will take effort. There are no magic spells to make you suddenly love reading your Bible and be super committed to it. Many a Bible reading plan were started on January 1 and ended in mid-February because it isn't always easy. We need to be aware so that we can press on.

It might be your testimony that you believed in Christ and fell in love with reading the Bible. If so, praise God for that! You should give God thanks for this gift, because it is a gift. This is not the case for everyone. Don't be surprised when you come across other students and adults in your church who do not fall into this category. It is difficult for many Christians.

It may be a fight to begin reading your Bible on a consistent basis. It often is. You will probably miss some days. However, it is a battle worth fighting. If this is how God has revealed Himself to us, and our greatest joy is found in knowing, loving, and obeying Him, then reading is the vehicle that brings us to more joy. Reading, understanding, and living the Bible is the window into a world of joy. The path may be filled with obstacles and pitfalls, but our commitment must remain because our God is worth it.

## KNOW YOURSELF

We will begin with 'when.' Each person is unique, and so tailoring the best times to read and study the Bible will largely be determined by what time you have available and when you are most sharp in your thinking. The best time for me to read the Bible may not be the best time for you. This means that any hard rule is not just impossible but will largely be unhelpful. As you probably have figured out, I am not a high school student, which means our days do not look the same. We need to recognize this if we are going to build sustainable habits. What you do may not work for your parents. When your pastor reads his Bible may not be the same as your Sunday school teacher. That is okay. We are all wired differently.

Reading the Bible is important. As Christians we want to know God in a deeper way and obey Him. We want to give God our best, and not serve Him the leftovers of our time and energy. This is what I mean when I say that we should determine when we are going to read based upon when we are most sharp in our thinking. God deserves our clearest thinking, and that time may look differently for each one of us. He deserves our best, not what we have left.

I will use myself as an example. Throughout my high school and college days I would read the Bible at night, right before I went to bed. This was the time when the house was quiet, and my roommate was usually settling down to go to bed. I could focus. I could think. I need quiet to think well. If there is a lot of background noise, then I struggle to focus. It is just the way I am wired. The nighttime proved to be the best time for it.

Except this has changed completely now. Since I have graduated school, gotten married, and had a daughter, my Bible reading time looks different. I am usually up earlier than my wife and daughter and read the Bible with a cup of coffee. This is completely opposite of what I was doing only a few years before. What changed? Life did. I needed to adjust in order to continue to focus on the Bible. My desire to know God has not changed. In fact, it has only grown. My circumstances have changed, and so I made a switch.

What made me change was that I could not focus at night. I would be reading and then my eyes would get tired. I would slowly start to close them and then, right before I was asleep, I would have to shake myself awake to finish the chapter. It was not productive at all. I was not actually reading. I was more of holding open the Bible and letting my eyes go across the page with little to no comprehension. This was not always the case, but it is now. So, I made the shift so I could give God my best.

You, on the other hand, might focus well at night. You might be in a sport and have to be up early and do not get home until late, so the only time you have open to read is late. That is fine. You need to know yourself and plan your day accordingly. It will be difficult to establish a pattern if you go against yourself. If you cannot wake up early well, then stay up a little later to read. If you fall asleep early, then wake up earlier to read. If neither work best, but you can read a bit in the afternoon, that is fine. Know yourself and make it a commitment. Strive to find out when you are most awake and alert. That is the time you give to God.

## STRIVE FOR CONSISTENCY

Rome wasn't built in a day. A masterpiece painting didn't happen at one sitting. Athletes aren't able to make a game winning shot in the face of intense defensive pressure with the clock winding down because they shot the ball from the same spot once in practice. Repetition and consistency are the key to growth in any discipline; it is the same for your understanding of the Bible. It is the consistent, day-after-day reading and studying that will yield the greatest results. We are building the house of our Christian life one brick at a time.

For some of us, like myself, this can be a difficult lesson to learn. All throughout my high school career I found that I did not need to study for the big test days or weeks ahead of time. I could study the night before and do pretty well on the test. I am naturally a good test-taker. It might work for a while, and in some subjects, but it will not always work (though you may have to learn the lesson the hard way first). It took a while to realize this weakness in my study habits.

I can say with absolute certainty that I married up. My wife is stunningly beautiful, incredibly sweet, smart, and out of my league. We met when she was a freshman in college, and I was a sophomore. She was studying to be a nurse, which is a very difficult major and field, if for no other reason than the sheer amount of information she needed to learn. You should really be thankful for this type of training the next time you go see your doctor. They did not enter the medical field because it was easy. It took time and effort.

When it came to classes and tests, our time in college was quite different. I was able to study and prepare for my tests a few days ahead of taking them. I was able to do well in my classes. My wife, on the other hand, could be found studying a week or more before her class because of how difficult her tests were. Don't get me wrong, my wife was a great student. This was just how hard the tests were, and to even stay in the program you had to maintain a B average on tests. The pressure was awful. She put in the work necessary to do well, and graduate early (did I mention I married up?).

If she tried to simply cram the night before the test, then she would not have done well and probably would not have graduated from nursing school. It took a consistent studying and pouring over her notes that allowed her to understand the material and do well on the test. It is the same when it comes to the Bible. We must be committed to reading and studying the Bible daily if we want to grow in our walk with Christ. A tree is not planted one day and then springs up and bears fruit the next. Little by little, it grows. The wall that will protect the city must be built one brick at a time. Your faithfulness to Christ throughout all your life and maturation in the faith will be built one opening of your

Bible upon another opening. We dig a little deeper, and the well will give more water.

After you have spent some time trying to think about when you are available and when you are sharp, the next step is to make a plan. Some individuals may not like having a plan because they believe that if we are just following a plan then it won't be genuine. That may be true for some. However, I think, as the saying goes, to fail to plan is to plan to fail.

Think of it like this. If you want to become a better musician, say playing the piano, then you will need a plan to improve. Simply saying you want to improve will never be enough if you don't make adjustments to your schedule. You will not get better if you wait for a spark of inspiration because there will be plenty of moments in which the desire is not there. You will still need to practice, whether you feel like it or not. If you were to commit, say, to one hour or practice three times a week, then, after a few months, you will be far better than when you started. The plan is a guideline to keep you on track, to help you stay committed when the desire is not there. Discipline comes in when desire is lacking.

For me, I need a plan. I have been using a variety of Bible reading plans for years.[1] The reason is simple: I like to know what to expect and make progress. If I don't have a plan, then I find myself scratching my head, wondering what I should read. A Bible reading plan is a tool that helps me in this area. Maybe you are more committed than I am, and a reading plan wouldn't help you. That is fine. But we still need some sort of a plan.

Think through a few questions to help establish a plan. Are you more awake at night or in the morning? Would it be better to get up a few minutes earlier so that you can read and pray before school? Do you have time and energy at night so that you can read before you go to bed? Would a daily plan help you stay on track? Are you less distracted using a physical Bible as opposed to reading on your phone? Answering these questions is a good first step.

This brings up one point that is necessary for us to consider. We live in a world of distraction. I am writing on a computer and have to constantly fight the urge to check Facebook, email, or even Amazon as I write. I am willing to bet that you know exactly what I am talking about. How many math problems have been interrupted for twenty minutes because you heard a ding from your phone and had to check it? How many papers took far longer than necessary because you had a TV show playing in the background? We crave distractions. This will not change when it comes to the Bible. If anything, because we are at war with cosmic powers and spiritual forces that do not want us to grow as a Christian, the craving for distraction will only increase (Eph. 6:12).

Because of this, we need to do our best to eliminate as many distractions as we possibly can. For me, when it comes time to study my Bible or prepare a lesson to teach, I usually will put my phone in a different room. If it is within arm's reach, then I will usually reach for it. If this isn't an option, then silence your phone or turn off notifications. We need to fight to focus because our relationship with God is the most important relationship in our lives. He is worth our full attention.

For example, say you are out to dinner with your best friend. You have been looking forward to this time because you both have been so busy that you haven't seen each other in a few weeks. You are ready to catch up and tell him all about what has been happening in your life. However, while you are talking, every few minutes your friend picks up his phone for a minute or so, and then sets it down. His eyes are constantly bouncing back-and-forth from you to his phone. This wouldn't lead you to think he was really listening. It might even give the impression that he doesn't want to be there at all. He cares far more about what is happening on his phone than he does what you are saying. This is hurtful.

If we wouldn't want this to happen at dinner with a friend, then why would we think it is okay to treat the God of the universe in this way. We can say that we love God and are following Christ, but are we even giving Him focused time in our days? We need to eliminate as many distractions as we can so that we can focus on the Word of God and the God of the Word.

For me, this looks like using a physical Bible. I am easily distracted on any technology, so it has to go when I read. I love my Bible. I like to mark it up. I love to take it to church and open it up as the pastor is preaching. Perhaps this will help you too. Get a Bible that you love. Pour over its pages. Fall in love with the Bible. Mark it up. Underline. Make notes. It is yours. A well-used and well-loved Bible is a beautiful sight. As Charles Spurgeon has said, "A Bible that is falling apart usually belongs to someone who isn't."

I know you are young, and your life will certainly change over the next few years after high school, whether that is going to college or getting a job. However, if you commit yourself to building the habit of reading your Bible regularly, and hopefully daily, then it will bring immense benefits in your relationship with God in the future. As a follower of Christ, we are to be committed to loving and obeying God for the entirety of our lives, and this includes when we are young. Don't waste the time you have now by putting off your Bible until you are older. God has so many amazing things to teach you and show you in the pages of Scripture, but you won't see any of them if you don't open it up. It is like having the sunset over the ocean, and you shut your eyes and miss it. It is a shame, really.

Commit yourself to the Bible. It is a lifelong project that will only be fully completed in eternity with Christ. However, you are facing a world that is increasingly hostile to God. You will not survive as a Christian without the lifeline of the Bible. The Bible is not just a helpful addition we add to our lives. It is our connection to reality as God has designed it. We need it far more than we realize. I don't say this lightly. You will not make it as a faithful follower of Christ without the Bible. There are far too many adversaries to try to go it alone. You need your church and the Bible.

Matt Smethurst provides a helpful example. In his book, *Before You Open Your Bible,* he speaks about approaching your Bible desperately. This was not something he imagined about Bible reading, until it became necessary. In college, he had a roommate that was ardently antagonistic toward Christianity, and Matt himself. He writes, "In order to survive the situation with [his roommate] I started reading my Bible. Devouring it, really. Perhaps the language of survival sounds a bit dramatic to you, but that's what it felt like to my eighteen-year-old self. I realized I couldn't survive a single day with [him] if I didn't begin the day with God. I wasn't approaching my Bible out of duty. I wasn't even approaching it out of delight. I was approaching it out of desperation."[2]

We may not ever be in the same situation as Matt, but our desperation for the Bible is the same. The sooner we can realize this the better prepared we will be. We are soldiers in the Lord's Army, combatting against the forces of darkness, and the lone offensive weapon we have is the sword of the Spirit, which is the Word of God (Eph. 6:17). We may not always feel it, but we need the Bible. This is where the commitment to God and His Word come in. When the desire to read is not there, we must remember the need we have, and the Treasure we receive in the Word. If we don't, then we will easily set it to the side when other needs arise. We cannot afford to do this.

Here is my plea to you: commit to reading your Bible. Commit to reading the entire Bible regularly. Read whole books and not just short sections. If you don't know where to start, then ask your parents or your pastor. I would recommend starting in a place like the Gospel of John so that you can get a sight of Jesus.

Take an inventory of your own life. What time do you have available? What are you willing to give up to make time for the Bible? Are you willing to give up twenty extra minutes of sleep to spend time with God? What app can you delete and give yourself some extra time? We have time if we are willing to plan well. When are you at your best? How can you eliminate distractions? How you can make a plan and stick to it, with the goal of building good habits that will help you for the rest of your life?

As we said earlier, a house is built one day at a time. I really believe that you will see growth in your love for the Lord and knowledge of His Word over the course of the next few months and years if you will commit yourself to reading the Bible. The more you know God, the more joy you will have in Him. He is the Treasure you were made to know and pursue. He is worth any time and effort that it takes. This is my promise to you. Start now, and we can thank God together in eternity for His faithfulness and grace in giving us the Scripture.

## A METHOD

Before we finish this chapter, I wanted to provide a method to help you study the Bible. I first learned this method from Robby Gallaty, while attending a conference in my city. It is a simple and helpful method entitled HEAR. HEAR is an acronym for highlight, explain, apply, and respond. This is one way that you may find beneficial as you seek to study the Bible. There are certainly other options as well, so if this one isn't for you, no hard feelings. It is just a way that could prove helpful.

This method works best when you are writing in a journal. This will allow you to follow the same pattern as you go through a book of the Bible. Plus, it allows you to read back over previous ones and not forget what the Lord was teaching you then. Here is a description of the method:

- Highlight. As you read through a particular passage or chapter, highlight one verse that stands out to you. Write it out in a journal.

- Explain. What is going on in this verse. We want to learn what Paul or John or whoever else is saying in this passage. What do these words mean? What is the context? What happens before? What happens after? In your own words, write out what you think is going on.

- Apply. How does this verse apply to your life? Is there something in this passage that you should be doing? Is Jesus spending time in prayer and you need to as well? How does this verse affect how you view your upcoming test? Be specific.

- Respond. What are you going to commit to do as a result of this passage? I would recommend writing out a prayer based on what you just read.

I have found this to be a helpful way to learn how to study the Bible, especially when someone is starting to study in a deeper way. Simply starting is crucial. There are also a few ideas that we need to keep in mind as we seek to study. These are important foundations that you will build upon for years to come.

First, the goal is to know our Triune God. This might be assumed for some of you, but I want to be clear. The goal is never head knowledge, but communion with our God that leads to obedience to Him. We get the joy of spending time with Him as we learn more about Him. He is the goal. We are seeking to taste and see that the Lord is good (Ps. 34:8). Enjoy God as you read the Bible. Our salvation rests in Christ, and eternal life is found in knowing the Father and His Son through the Spirit (Jn. 17:3).

Secondly, understanding the Bible happens when we understand what the author meant. The author has a meaning in mind as he writes. Our job is to discover the meaning. We don't like it when people put words in our mouths that we have never said. We cannot do that for the biblical authors either. Paul uses the words that he does for a reason. What is he saying? Words matter. Sentences matter. Grammar might not be your favorite subject in school, but it will help you know God. Don't neglect basic reading comprehension when it comes to the Scripture. We understand what a text means only when we understand what the author meant in the text. This is not application. We will get there. This is our seeking to understand meaning. Meaning doesn't change.

Along with this, there is the golden rule of context: context rules. Look at what happens before and after a text in order to understand why the author says what he does. A major example of this is Philippians 4:13, "I can do all things through him who strengthens me." I have seen quite a few athletes wear this on their eye black before a football game. Is that Paul's point, though? Is he saying that, through Jesus, we can win the big game? No. in the context, Paul is speaking about enduring anything, whether it is poverty or prosperity, because Jesus is better and gives him strength. He can endure hunger and abundance through Jesus. That is different than trying to win a game.

Thirdly, application happens after we understand what the text means. We cannot apply something we don't comprehend. Application is important. I want to know how the text applies to my life. What we want to know first, though, is what the text actually means. If we get this order wrong, then we can get into some pretty weird places. Meaning will be the same for everyone. Application will be unique to you.

The best method for starting to read the Bible is whatever will help you read the Bible. If the HEAR method looks interesting, give it a shot with the gospel of John. Take a chapter a day and read over it. Pick out one verse or passage to highlight. If it is not for you, then find another option. I love Bible reading plans. They have helped me tremendously. In either case, start reading and studying. Strive for consistency. Take your time. Be willing to ask questions when you don't understand. Remember, the goal is to know, love, and serve God in a deeper way.

## CHAPTER ENDNOTES

[1] The YouVersion app has some wonderful options to get started. My current plan is entitled the Discipleship Journal Reading Plan, and it will take you through the entire Bible in a year. It allows five days at the end of each month to catch up on any days you have missed too. I recommend searching through the plans on this app to get started.

[2] Matt Smethurst, *Before You Open Your Bible: Nine Heart Postures for Approaching God's Word* (Leyland, England: 10 Publishing, 2019), 22.

# Chapter 3:
## The Gospel and Evangelism

Imagine for a minute that you are on a trip to the safari in Africa. You have an excellent guide that has been able to show you all of the unique features of the landscape. He points out all of the different types of vegetation, the sources of water for each, and animals that you will see. He talks about the lizards that are laying on the rocks, enjoying the sun while you are sweating through your shirt. He describes the elephants and giraffes and the mighty lion, that can sneak up and attack unsuspecting gazelles. You are gripped by the sights and sounds of your trip.

Except, now the jeep is slowing down and coming to a stop. The guide is keeping his cool and telling you it is just a small delay, and we will be back on the trip quickly. Then, after an hour, then two, then three, you start to get a little nervous. The sun is starting to go down and it will be dark soon. Will you be stuck out here all night? You didn't even want to come on this trip at all. You wanted to stay at the resort, and now you might be spending the night in the safari.

By this time, the Jeep is empty, and the guests are just sitting in a circle. Since you know by now that you will be spending the night outside under the stars, you decide that you are going to be helpful and gather sticks to build a fire. After all, you will feel much better about this night if there is a warm fire to sit around, and hopefully get a little sleep. You're not convinced sleep is anywhere in your near future though. It is going to be a long night, and everyone knows it.

You head a few yards away from the make-shift campsite in order to start picking up sticks; then a little further; then further still. You can still see the Jeep, but you aren't really close any longer. You are bending down to pick up a few solid sticks that will be perfect for the fire when you hear a soft rustle coming from the taller grass. You did just feel a breeze on your sunburnt face, so it was probably nothing. Then you hear another. Now your heart is racing. You begin to sweat. You need to make a break for the camp, but the moment you turn around, you are now face-to-face with a full-size adult lion, ready to have his dinner.

What is the point of that story? Well, when it comes to sharing the gospel with those closest to us, many of us are less afraid of the lion. We would much rather face this hungry beast then to open our mouths and talk about God, sin, Jesus, the cross, and the need to respond in faith and repentance.

Sharing the gospel is a discipline, and one of the hardest we need to develop as followers of Christ. I will confess that I am still not the most comfortable with this discipline. What I do know, and what I long for you to know and believe, is that it is simpler than you probably think.

## It's Not on You

I want to say something from the outset that is incredibly important. You need to understand this if you are going to be confident in your sharing the gospel: God saves sinners. You do not. Now, exhale. The pressure is not on you to convert your friends or family members. As much as you long for them to believe in Christ, you cannot save them. That is not your job, nor do you have the power to do it. However, what you can do is tell them about the One who can, and who has died in the place of sinners and rose again in order to do just that. We need to understand that our role is to share good news. God will do the rest. As J. I. Packer so clearly writes, "While we must always remember that it is our responsibility to proclaim salvation, we must never forget that it is God who saves."[1]

This dual reality is important for us to understand as followers of Christ. We cannot pretend that we have the power or authority to convert anyone to Christ. We cannot open the eyes of the blind (2 Cor. 4:4), raise the dead (Eph. 2:1), or make someone love what they hate (Jn. 3:19). No matter how much you want to, how clear your words are, how often you share, you don't have that power, and that is actually really good news for us. We could not handle that weight. We would buckle under the pressure[2] because we were never designed to bear it. Take heart. God saves.

What this does not do, though, is absolve us of our responsibility to actively share the gospel with our friends, family members, or neighbors. God, in His grace, has given Christians the wonderful privilege of sharing the wonderful news of the gospel to those who desperately need to hear it. Without the gospel, every single individual is guilty before God and will earn the wages of sin, which is death (Rom. 6:23). This is why evangelism is so important, and why I long for you to build this discipline into your life now. Eternity is on the line. Heaven and hell are at stake. We cannot be lazy. This is too important to neglect.

Let me illustrate the situation because words like 'eternity' can seem pretty abstract. Say you have a friend that is asleep in a house, like any other night. He is all tucked in and sound asleep. It is early in the night, and you are driving home from getting a late-night snack and you notice smoke coming from the direction of your friend's house. Naturally, you head that way to investigate. When you pull up to his house you see flames beginning to engulf the entire house. It will only be a few minutes before the house collapses with your friend inside. With the little time that you have, what are you going to do?

The most loving act you can do in this moment is to burst open the door and warn your friend that his house is on fire. In fact, that is the only loving thing you can do. You must warn him of the danger that is slowly making its way through the house. If you call him and wake him up, he may not believe you that his house is on fire. He may think you are kidding and just go back asleep, but you must keep reaching out to him. You don't want him to perish in the house fire. You must warn him. It would be the height of hate to do otherwise.

This is the position every believer finds himself in when it comes to evangelism. The unbeliever must be warned about the very real danger of being under the wrath of God. They may not sense the danger right now, like the friend who doesn't believe his house is no fire because he cannot see the flames. This does not change the truth. We must warn those around us. We have that responsibility from God. We cannot save; but we can warn. We can announce. We can share. We can call to repent and believe.

## Gospel Message, Simply Put

I really believe every Christian knows sharing the gospel is important. The reason we often don't share is because we are unclear on what to say. Understandably, we don't often speak up when we are unsure of what we should say. We feel awkward, like being called on in class when we don't know the answer to the question. Most of the time, we just keep our heads down and hope the teacher overlooks us. We might feel convicted about not sharing the gospel with our friends, and we might even see some openings where we could share, but we don't because we aren't sure how to express it. The spirit is willing, but the flesh is weak (Mt. 26:41).

I want to help with this by laying out the gospel message in five simple categories that you can share with those around you. If we can know these five stages well, we will be able to confidently explain the gospel to someone in a clear and concise manner. We want to keep it short and sweet. Those categories are: God, man, sin, Christ, and response. Another way of saying this is by asking: where did everything come from; why were we made; what went wrong; how can it be fixed; what must we do in response? If we ask these questions, it will help solidify our understanding of our good news and help others see the need for Jesus.

## GOD

Everything begins and ends with God. He is the Creator of everything. All things are from Him and through Him and to Him (Rom. 11:36). He is the glorious God who rules over all things. He has all authority. He is almighty. He is the One by whom we were made and for whom we were made. We owe our lives to Him. If we are going to share the gospel with someone, then we must tell them clearly who God is. One of the clearest depictions of God we have in Scripture is found in Isaiah 6. This shatters our cozy picture of a small god that lives to serve us and brings us into the presence of the true God of the universe. If we can become gripped with this image of God, then we will have confidence to share the gospel with our friends.

I highly recommend that you stop reading this book and go read Isaiah 6. We will not be able to hit every wonderful detail in this scene, but it will be well worth your time to think about what it would be like to come into the throne room of God. Isaiah 6:1 says, "In the year that King Uzziah died I saw the Lord sitting upon a throne, high and lifted up". In the year that the king has died, the true King is still alive and well. In the time when the throne has been vacated, the throne of heaven is still occupied. He is not going anywhere.

This remains true today. Every four years in the United States, we have the opportunity to vote upon who will be the President. We have the potential to have someone new every four years. It can be hard to keep track after a while. I certainly cannot tell you every President in our history. The wonderful reality is, no matter who is President, God is still King. This will never change.

His throne is high and lifted up. He is above everything. Being up high is a sign of power and authority. He is overseeing the entire creation. If you were to have an office in a big city, would you rather be on the second floor or the tenth floor? Would you rather have an apartment on the ground level or the penthouse? To be up high is to have everything below you. We are awed when we see tall mountains and skyscrapers because we intuitively understand the significance of height as symbolizing grandeur. There is no one or nothing higher than God.

God is high and lifted up. The entire universe is under his feet, both symbolically and literally. No one is higher. He is secure in this position. No one can take His seat from Him. He is not nervously pacing the throne room because the world isn't going the way that He wants it to go. He is seated. He is in control.

This is true whether we like it or not. God does not cease to be sitting on His throne because someone does not believe in God. That would be like saying the sun is not really shining because a blind man cannot see it. Someone may have arguments against God, but this does not change truth. Truth is true in all places, at all times. God is reigning. He has been reigning from eternity past and will be reigning into eternity future. Christian, you have every reason to be confident when you share the gospel because your God is on the throne.

Not only is He powerful and authoritative, He is holy. In fact, He is holy, holy, holy. If there is one book that has helped me, outside of the Bible, to see the holiness of God it is *The Holiness of God* by R. C. Sproul.[3] God has used this book in major ways over my last ten years. If we are going to understand why we desperately need Jesus, and why we need to be willing to share Jesus with those around us, then we need to understand that God is holy.

When we think of holiness, we often think of moral purity. We think of our own struggles and then put the opposite back on God. We struggle with lust, which is unholy. Therefore, holiness must mean purity. We struggle with gossiping and talking bad about someone behind his or her back. This isn't holy. God, therefore, must be pure in this way. We take the opposite of sin and put it back on God. But moral purity doesn't cover totally what it means for God to be holy.

Sproul writes, "the point we must remember is that the idea of the holy is never exhausted by the idea of purity. It includes purity but is much more than that. It is purity and transcendence. It is a transcendent purity."[4] Transcendence means God is above us. God is not just a more righteous version of us; He definitely is that, but He is so much more. He is of an entirely different kind. He is the Creator, and we are the creature. He is above us. He is not just a bigger or stronger version, like a Superman. He is wholly other.

This reality can shake us to our core because the more we understand the greatness of God, the more we can see ourselves rightly. We can feel pretty good about ourselves so long as we compare ourselves to other humans. This changes when we compare ourselves to God. When we understand in small part who God is, then we are finally able to see ourselves rightly, just like Isaiah did when he beheld God. To this scene, we will return.

### HUMANITY

Why does it matter for your teammate to believe in Jesus? Why is spending eternity with God important (other than avoiding hell at all costs)? Would we even want this if the alternative was not quite so bad? This is where talking about our original design is so important. We were made to be in a relationship with God. This is where we flourish. When we share the gospel, we need to tell people their original purpose, and to do that we must start at the beginning.

Genesis 1 is a chapter full of beginnings. The beginning of everything, actually. The beginning of the world, time, animals, and the Bible. The narrative moves quickly as God creates everything. He creates the mountains, the sky, the water, animals, fruits, and vegetables. Anything that exists does so because God created it. How amazing is that! Our God created everything, and He did it by His word.

Stop and think about that for a second. Test it for yourself. Yell out, "let there be..." and see if whatever you want comes into being. I can guarantee you that it won't, unless you yell out for a snack and your loving mother hears you and brings it to you. In that case, you are not powerful but spoiled. This is what I meant when I said God is different from us. He has the power to create by His word. He speaks a word and things happen. Worlds are made. Stars start shining. If you have been in church for a while and are familiar with it, then my prayer is that you will be blown away afresh by this. It is stunning.

All of creation takes place in a matter of twenty-five verses, but then comes to a screeching halt when humanity is created. The story slows way down. How interesting is that? It is almost as if the Author wants us to pay close attention to what is about to take place. This is an important moment that we cannot miss.

We see this often in our movies and television shows. A large period of time can be overlooked or past over without much mention because we need to pay attention to the really important part. Think of the movie *Shrek*, for example. When Shrek and Donkey begin their quest to rescue Princess Fiona for Lord Farquaad, they have to travel over a great distance. We get to watch a montage of the different terrain that they cover on along the way, but this journey takes only a few minutes before they arrive at the rope bridge to the dragon-guarded castle. The point was not that the journey was unimportant, but rather the scene that was beginning was more important. The emphasis is on the rescue, not on the trip.

God creating the universe is really important. The symmetry and order are staggering. All of the animals are beautiful and worth mentioning in detail, but the narrative leads us to the moment where humanity is created. The other details are not irrelevant. We are just meant to pay attention to the uniqueness of humanity.

Check out what God does before He creates humanity. Genesis 1:26-27 says, "Then God said, 'Let us make man in our image, after our likeness. And let them have dominion over the fish of the sea and over the birds of the heavens and over the livestock and over all the earth and over every creeping thing that creeps on the earth.' God created man in His own image, in the image of God He created him; male and female He created them." Before He creates humanity He has an intra-Trinitarian conversation. How cool is that? The Father, Son, and Holy Spirit discuss the creation of humanity before it happens. This did not happen before the sun was made, Mount Everest was placed, or the lion made his first roar; and yet, it happened before humanity. We are His special creation. Unlike the rest of the universe, we are made in His image.

What exactly does it mean to be made in the image of God? We are not completely sure, at least I am not completely sure. What I do know is that we are unique. No other creature was made in this way. The personal touch of breathing into Adam's nostril after forming him out of the dirt is astounding (Gen. 2:7). We have reason. We can think and articulate those thoughts. We have language and can communicate with God and with one another. We have a conscience. We feel deeply right and wrong, what ought to be done and what ought not to happen. We are His special creation, and we were made to be in a relationship with Him.

We were made in His image in order to image Him to the world. We were to show off how great God is by filling the world with image-bearers. We were to have dominion over the world as His representative. He left us in charge of the world He made. We were made to build cities and culture and make the world flourish, all for the glory of God. This was not a task that was given to squirrels. Killer whales were not designed to have dominion over the lions of the Sahara. Humanity was given this role. This is our purpose. We are to commune with God and image Him forth to the rest of creation.

Unfortunately, this has been forgotten by many in our world. There is an angst in our world right now in the pursuit of purpose. We long to know why we are here. You may have even wondered this too. These are not questions that are reserved for the ivory-tower philosophers. We have social media pages filled with people looking for a purpose. There are thousands of self-help books available. We crave the meaning, and many don't know where to look. The world is in the dark, groping about, and searching for answers.

The wonderful news of Christianity is that we know our purpose. We have the light, not because we are smarter and figured it out, but because God has given us His Word. Paul makes it clear in Romans 11:36, when he writes, "For from him and through him and to him are all things. To him be glory forever. Amen." The point of everything, and the point of our individual lives, is the glory of God. We were made for Him. We will flourish when we live in His design.

When you share the gospel with someone, you are sharing with them the good news of how to be restored to the One for whom they have been made. Every single person has been made to be in a relationship with God. Every single one is made in the image of God and designed to image Him forth. When you share the gospel, you are seeking to restore the purpose for which they were created. No matter who you have the chance to share with, this will always be true.

However, before we get to communion with God restored, something happened in order to disrupt our relationship with God. We need to know what happened before we can give the answer to how to fix it. We must give the problem before we can show the solution. We call this devastating moment 'the Fall'. Sin enters the picture and wrecks this harmony between Creator and creature.

## Sin

We can read the first two chapters of Genesis and struggle to imagine what it would be like because it is far from what we experience in our everyday life. That type of peace and harmony, literally walking with God in the garden, seems more imaginary than the original reality. It is hard to believe. This is because we live in a world that is fractured by sin.

This is perhaps the most uncomfortable aspect of sharing the gospel with someone you know and love. You must tell them that they are a sinner. Regardless of how outwardly good she is, she is still a sinner before God. How do I know this to be the case? It is because, apart from Jesus, this person will never obey God as she was called to do. It is because of the command that undergirds every other command in the Bible. This command is found in 1 Corinthians 10:31, in which Paul declares, "So, whether you eat or drink, or whatever you do, do all to the glory of God."

Outwardly, someone might be an incredibly nice person. She can be kind, considerate, and generous with his time and resources. We might like this person. We may enjoy hanging out with her. You probably have someone in mind right now that fits this profile. She is just a great person. However, apart from believing in Christ, she is not living for the glory of God. Therefore, even her best acts are tinged with sin. She is still guilty because she is still not completely obeying. To only obey halfway is to disobey. The holiness of God demands complete obedience and does not grant partial credit when it comes to righteousness.

Have you ever walked into a house of someone who used to smoke a lot? It still smells like smoke. He may not have touched a cigarette in years, but the scent remains. It will always be there. You can replace the carpet and change the furniture, paint the walls and get all new appliances, but the scent will remain. In a similar way, no matter how much good we think we are doing, apart from Christ, we are still sinners. It will always be a part of who we are, no matter how much 'progress' we have made on our own.

Genesis 3 is the explanation as to why the world is in the state that it is in. The creation has been cursed by God as a result of the disobedience of our first parents, Adam and Eve. They failed to trust the word of God, gave into the temptation of the serpent, and we are still reaping the consequences all these years later. Suffering, cancer, natural disasters, death, relational conflict, and separation from God are a result of the Fall. We are all guilty before God. What are the wages for our sin? Death (Rom. 6:23). Not only physical death, but also eternal death in hell. This is what awaits every sinner. Every single person is a sinner (Rom. 3:10-11, 23). No one, apart from Jesus, is exempt.

This is why we are to be bold in sharing the gospel. If we are left to ourselves, we will die. In fact, we deserve to die. We are guilty before God. It is right for Him to judge us. We cannot redeem ourselves. We cannot do enough good works in order to cover over our sin.

Say you are a judge in a court case. You are listening to the testimony of a person who has been convicted of murdering a person. He has readily admitted that he has committed the crime. He planned it and carried it out. He is guilty. However, to your surprise, when it comes time to cast the sentence, he starts to tell you about all of the good things he has done. He helped an older neighbor bring in her groceries. He gave a homeless man some money. He rescued a cat out of a tree. He tells you all about these acts because he wants you to let him off for the murder. He's a good person, he pleads, he only killed the one person.

Now, if you were the judge, would you let him off the hook? The answer should be no. He should not be let off because of the good works. Why? It is because he is still guilty of the crime. None of those actions, or any other deed for that matter, can change the fact that he is a murderer. As a just judge, you rightly condemn him. So, it is with our case before God. As we saw in the first step, God is infinitely holy. Because He is infinitely holy, He will be just. Therefore, we are condemned. This is fair. This is right. It cannot be otherwise.

No amount of good can cover even one sin, let alone the thousands that we have committed in our lives. We are in a terrible situation. We are in a hopeless situation if God doesn't intervene. I hope you didn't miss the pronoun: we. Every single person, myself included, is guilty before God. We all need a Savior. This is the bad news that leads us to share the good news.

## CHRIST

Enter Jesus Christ. It is only after we have talked about the holiness of God, our creation to be with Him, and the entrance of sin that we can clearly talk about Jesus. If we jump straight to Jesus without first telling someone about sin, it would be like trying to convince someone to take medicine without diagnosing them of a disease. It would seem odd. If they are not in danger, then a Savior is not necessary. We need to tell them the problem and then the solution. Jesus is the solution. Sin is the problem.

Jesus is not like anyone else who has ever lived. There are many who would like to portray Him as another great moral teacher or social revolutionary, but this is not what we see in Scripture. Throughout the Gospels, we see Jesus portrayed as God in the flesh. He is the Word made flesh (Jn. 1:1-4, 14). He is Immanuel, God with us (Mt. 1:23). He and the Father are one (Jn. 10:30). He is truly God and truly man. He is sinless (2 Cor. 5:21). He is unique. He alone is able to save.

From His conception by the Holy Spirit, being born of a virgin, to His ministry and sinless life, to His death on the cross and subsequent resurrection, Jesus had a single, all-consuming mission from God. Jesus makes this clear when He says, "For even the Son of Man came not to be served but to serve, and to give his life as a ransom for many" (Mk. 10:45). This is what Jesus came to do. He came to give His life as a ransom.

What comes to mind when you hear the word 'ransom'? if you are like me, then it is probably an old action movie in which someone kidnaps the child of a wealthy person and is holding him hostage until money is paid. If the kidnapper gets the million dollars, then the child will be returned safely. This is the ransom needed for the child to be saved. If you give the money, you will get the child safe-and-sound. The police are working hard to talk down the criminals throughout. Usually by the end of the movie though, the kidnapper is arrested, and the child is returned thanks to the hero. Usually predictable, but enjoyable, nonetheless.

A ransom is a payment given in exchange for someone else. It is a price paid to redeem someone or something. This is what Jesus came to do. He came to give His life in order to be a payment for 'many'. The many are those who believe in Him. All Christians are included in this. One question arises we need to answer: how could His life be given in exchange for ours? The answer to this is found in the sinlessness of Christ and His perfect obedience.

Imagine you decide to buy your first car. You have waited and studied and finally passed your driver's test. It is awesome. You can go anywhere you want to go. The problem is you don't have a car. You have to rely on your parents letting you drive the family car, and that really isn't your style. So, you decide to get a job and save up some money in order to put a down payment on a vehicle of your own. You head to the bank and sign a loan. You are excited, but you are now in debt.

The year keeps going, you keep working to pay for the car. However, now that the calendar has turned, you are preparing to play the sport that you love. It is a huge time commitment, especially when classes are becoming harder. Something has got to give, and it looks like the job is only option. The problem with this is you are still in debt. You still owe money. That debt hasn't changed just because you no longer want to work.

You are at a loss on what to do. You will only get to play this sport for another year or two, and then probably never again. You don't want to waste the opportunity. Grades are important, so you cannot slack off schoolwork. You cannot give up the job. The debt is too much, and you will lose the car if you don't continue to work the same number of hours. You are stuck.

It is just then your uncle tells you that he will pay off the car for you because he loves you and wants to support you. He knows how hard it is to balance school, sports, and a job. He has been there and wants to help you. How is it that he can do this? You owe the money. He doesn't. In order for him to make the payment, a few things need to happen. First, he needs to have the money to pay. If he cannot afford it, then his generosity is nice, but unhelpful. Secondly, he has to assume the debt himself. Since you cannot pay, he will stand in your place before the bank. He pays the debt, and you get the car. He took on the charge so that you no longer owe. Thirdly, he pays the debt himself. He writes the check, and the check clears. He paid it, and you are now debt free.

In order for sinners to be freed from guilt, payment must be made. God cannot be righteous and forgive us without a payment. If sin were not punished, God would be unjust. Jesus is able to make this payment because He lived a sinless life (Heb. 4:15). He never incurred guilt to His account. Along with this, He perfectly kept the law. He had a righteousness of His own that He shares with His people. Both are needed. It is not helpful to simply not be sinful, that would only make us neutral. What we need is for a Savior to be perfectly righteous. Jesus was and is. He takes on our debt and can pay it in full.

At the cross, an exchange occurs. Jesus takes on the sin of His people and pays the debt that they owe. The guilt of sin is punished in Him. In this wonderful exchange, Jesus not only takes our penalty, He also gives us His righteousness. This is what Paul means when he says, "For our sake he made him to be sin who knew no sin, so that in him we might become the righteousness of God" (2 Cor. 5:21). He has not only gone to the bank to pay our debt, but then added our name to His account. His money is now our money. His righteousness is now our righteousness. His Sonship is our adoption. For those who are in Christ, for those who believe, we are justified. We are declared righteous before God.

How do we know the payment was successfully made? Just because your uncle sent a check to the bank for the correct amount does not mean the debt has been paid. What if the check bounces? We know the payment has been accepted because Jesus was raised on the third day. Everything rises and falls on the resurrection. Death is the consequence for sin, and since Jesus was sinless, death had no hold on Him (Acts 2:24). When He was raised from the dead, our justification is secured (Rom. 4:25). Without the resurrection, we are without hope. With the resurrection though, we are saved.

This is the wonderful news of the gospel. Sinners can be brought back to the relationship for which we have been made because Christ died and rose again. The wrath of God rightly due for sin has been satisfied by Jesus, so now we can be forgiven. We are no longer guilty before Him. We are free to have the relationship with God we were made to have. It is all because of the work of Christ on our behalf. The salvation we offer others when we share the gospel is not based on what they need to do in order to earn everlasting life with God but is the declaration of what God has already done in Christ Jesus to redeem us. Christianity is not about our earning or deserving but about what Jesus has done. When Jesus declared from the cross, "It is finished", He meant it (Jn. 19:30).

## RESPONSE

What must our response be to this wonderful news? Our response is to repent and believe. When we repent, we are confessing our sin to God, declaring our absolute need for His mercy and grace, and turning away from sin. There is no salvation without recognizing our need. We are not coming to bargain with God. We are submitting to Him. We are trusting in Christ alone for our salvation. We are abandoning our sin and are committed to fighting against it for the rest of our lives. At the same time that we turn from our sin, we also turn toward Jesus in trust. We are placing our hope squarely on Him.

At the moment when we believe, we are justified before God. It is not our working, but our faith in Jesus that saves (Eph. 2:8–9). God has established faith as the vehicle to take us to salvation. Why is it? It is because, when we trust in Jesus, we are resting everything on Him. The praise of salvation is given only to God. Faith, not our works or what we do, is the instrument God uses to bring us to Jesus.

Say, for instance, you are climbing down a mountain. You are out on the side of the mountain, and nothing is holding you but a rope tied to an anchor at the top. Holding the rope is like faith, it is only useful when the object attached to it is secure. If you were to grip tightly to the rope and there is no anchor, then you would fall with the rope firmly in your hand. If the foundation is secure, you are secure.

Christ is our anchor. His finished work on the cross and in the resurrection is the basis for our hope. In Christianity, the goal is never to just believe more, but rather to trust in Jesus. To have faith in faith is useless. To have faith in Jesus is salvation. We are believing in Jesus. We are trusting in Him. We are banking our eternity on Him alone. This is our only hope. The precious promise we have received is that those who believe will not perish but have everlasting life (Jn. 3:16). This is what we believe ourselves and is what we share with all who will listen.

We must call others to repent and believe. This can be uncomfortable because you are telling them they are a sinner and must believe in someone else to be saved. However, the Bible is clear that if we confess with our mouth that Jesus is Lord and believe in our heart that God raised Him from the dead, we will be saved (Rom. 10:9). When we share, we are to convey the message and give them a chance to respond. The good news is only good news if we hear the gospel, repent of sin, and believe in the Lord Jesus Christ the crucified, risen, and returning Son of God. We must be united to Jesus by faith. This is the only way we are saved.

We will never outgrow repentance and faith. There is far more to living the Christian life than just repenting and believing that first time. Our lives are to be characterized by continual repentance and trust as we grow in our walk with Jesus. We are to live in obedience to Him in communion with other believers. We never graduate from the gospel. We go ever deeper into it. This is part of what it means to follow Jesus. However, at this moment, we are calling the person to repent and believe in Christ.

### Now What?

You may be wondering why so much space was dedicated to the gospel when the chapter is on evangelism. That is because we will not be able to share the gospel well with those around us if we are confused about the content of the gospel. We are heralds of our King. If we aren't sure of the message, then people will not be helped. This is why we went down this path together. We cannot help others down a road we have never traveled.

The order was not accidental. You might not encounter many people today who are looking for arguments for the existence of God. You are likely to meet people who want to know if they have purpose. They want to know why they are here in the first place. You can be the one to usher them into the presence of God and tell them the reason for their existence. This is the most loving and practical message you could ever share. It gives people real hope. The best part is that it is true. Jesus really did die and really did rise from the grave. Our hope doesn't end here. It carries into the next life where we will spend our eternity with our great God and Savior. You could be the instrument God uses to save another soul. How amazing would that be? What could be more important than this?

As we close, I want to leave you with some tips you may find helpful in your desire to share the gospel:

- Pray for the individual by name. If you want to share the gospel with someone, whether a family member or friend, pray for them by name. Ask God to give you opportunities to share with them. God may use this to open your eyes to the opportunities that are already around you. There are always opportunities, but we usually miss them because we are not looking. We will also have far more love and compassion for someone for whom we have prayed. James tells us we do not have because we do not ask (Jam. 4:2). Why not ask for the salvation of the ones you love? God honors such prayers.

- Ask good questions and listen. We want to build a relationship with the individual and show we care. This is far more likely when we take our relationship out of the superficial realm and into real life. Trust me, I know how easy it is to talk about sports and the weather with others. However, that is not helpful. Ask the person to tell you his story; and then listen well. Ask good questions and try to get to know them. What is his home life? What does he want to do for a career? What does he value in life? Are there ways you can pray for him? How can Christ be brought into the conversation naturally?

- Strive to live in holiness (even imperfectly). The worst indictment we can receive from an unbeliever is for that person to not even know we are a Christian. It will sound odd to hear about Jesus from someone whom you could not even tell was a believer. Far more people reject Christianity because of how they see Christians living than because of the claims of Christ, at least in my experience. How we live and what we say matters. We are not perfect, and it is not fair to be expected to be. What we are to be though, is striving to live in holiness, just like Jesus. We have been forgiven of sin, not to continue to live in sin, but to put it to death. When we are living for Jesus in what we watch, how we treat people, how we spend our time and money, then people may be more interested. Genuine love for Jesus and life change may be attractive to someone who is far from God.

- Talk about God regularly. Our conversations should be littered with talking about God. This shouldn't be in a cheesy, mechanical, forced way. We will naturally talk about what we love. You won't have to force me to talk about my wife and daughters, or my church, or my favorite baseball team. They will naturally flow out. If we talk to others about what God is teaching us in our Bible reading, or at church, then they might just listen when we tell them who this God is.

- Follow up at a later time. If they have questions that you don't know the answer to, then don't feel bad. It happens to all of us. Go, find the answer from a trusted source, and follow up at a later time. We don't want to forget about the opportunity. Along with this, if the conversation is interrupted, seek to pick it up at a later time. This is too important to let go. They will feel like you really care when you tell them you would like to continue the conversation later. It will show how much it matters to you.

- Know how to define success. Success in sharing the gospel is sharing the gospel.[5] We are not responsible for saving anyone. That is far above our pay grade. God alone can save. He calls us to be faithful and share. We are heralds delivering a message. We are not the King. If someone believes, praise God. If someone rejects the offer, then don't be discouraged. You can keep trying and move to someone else. A person might not believe on the first hearing but might on the tenth. You never know what God will do. It is easy to feel rejected personally. We must remember that they are not rejecting us, but Jesus. We keep going.

Any effort in sharing the gospel with others will not be wasted. I praise God for that. I pray that God will raise up a generation of Christians who know the gospel clearly and will share it boldly with those around them. Who knows? God may see fit to bring about a massive revival because you are willing to share the gospel with those around you. That is my prayer for you and for me. We want to see God glorified and sinners saved. There is nothing like seeing someone go from death to life when they repent and believe. I pray you will see it often in your life!

## Chapter Endnotes

[1] J. I. Packer, *Evangelism and the Sovereignty of God* (Downers Grove, IL: IVP Books, 2012), 32.

[2] Unlike Luisa in *Encanto*

[3] R. C. Sproul, *The Holiness of God* (Wheaton, IL: Tyndale House Publishers, 1998).

[4] Ibid. 48.

[5] Shoutout to my pastor, Daniel Palmer, for this phrase from a sermon preached at North Roanoke Baptist Church on January 1, 2023.

# Chapter 4:
## Prayer

What if you had the opportunity to talk to your hero, whether that be an athlete, an actor, a writer, a politician, or maybe even a pastor? Would you take the opportunity? I sure would. I would cherish the chance to sit down and pick the brain of some of the people I most admire. That would be an absolute dream come true.

What if I told you I could make it happen? I can arrange for you to spend time with your hero, and this person actually wants to talk to you. In all his busyness, he is going to make talking to you a priority, and not just once, but as often as you would like. He will give you his personal cell phone number, and you can call him as often as you would like. Any time you have a question, he is available for help. That sounds amazing, right?

Here is the catch. You have to have the same conversation every time you sit down with the person. Every phone call will begin and end in the same way, day after day. It might be exciting at first. You get to learn from this amazing person. The second and third time would probably still be okay. You might pick up on something he said that you didn't notice or had forgotten. However, after a while, it would start to get boring. You would dread picking up the phone or meeting up for lunch. Without any variety in the conversation, you would lose interest, no matter how awesome the other person is.

This is how prayer feels for many of us. We know we need to pray. We know it is important. We might even understand the privilege of getting to speak to the God of the universe, and yet we don't often make it a priority. We often neglect it. One reason for this is, if we are willing to be honest, we often find prayer to be boring (are pastors allowed to say that out loud?).

Just so we are clear, I am not perfect when it comes to prayer. This is an area of spiritual discipline that I still need to improve upon. I want you to know that in advance so that you can read what follows not as from someone who has 'arrived' or is an expert in this area, but rather someone who is struggling along just as you might be. We are in this together. Prayer is incredibly important, and I want to help you as best I can as I strive to grow in this myself. Maybe, by the end, we will both benefit.

## JESUS PRIORITIZED PRAYER

I mentioned in chapter 1 how I will often ask the question "what did Jesus think?" when approaching a variety of topics. The wrist band has taught me well. So, what did Jesus think about prayer? Since Jesus is our Lord and Savior, and since His priorities were always right, we should rightly seek to know how He approached prayer in His own ministry. Whatever He does will be the right course for us to take. Was it something that He viewed as important? Was prayer something that He made time to do? Was it a priority?

When you read through the Gospels carefully, you will see Jesus taking time away to be with His Father in prayer, and especially before milestone moments. When Jesus knew that a major event was about to take place, He would purposefully get away from the crowds that He might pray. If the Son of God needed to pray, how much more do we need to pray?

Take, for instance, Jesus selecting His twelve disciples in Luke 6. Luke records these words, "In these days he went out to the mountain to pray, and all night he continued in prayer to God. And when day came, he called his disciples and chose from them twelve." On the night before Jesus chooses His twelve disciples, a rather important choice I think we can all agree, He spent the night in prayer. He wanted to commune with the Father and be full of the Spirit before selecting those who were to be closest to Him for His three-year ministry. When was the last time you spent an entire night in prayer when an important decision needed to be made? He saw prayer as more important to His life and ministry than sleep. He took time away in order to pray.

The same can be said at the end of His ministry on earth. On the night that Jesus was betrayed, He led His disciples to a garden. Do you remember what the disciples were to do in Gethsemane? They were to pray. This is what Jesus asked them to do. What happened? Jesus prayed while the disciples fell asleep (Lk. 22:39-46). In His agony, sweating drops of blood in anticipation of bearing the wrath of God on the cross, Jesus prayed.

More examples could be mentioned, including the not-so-infrequent statements of Jesus going to be alone in order to pray. He understood the temple to be a place of prayer, even when the Jews had turned it into a place of business (Mt. 21:13). He flipped over tables and ran the merchants out because He valued prayer. Throughout His earthly life, Jesus leaves us an example of prioritizing spending time with the Father through prayer. Our issue is not that Jesus is unclear, but that we don't listen. Our problem is desire. Our problem is we often find it boring. Certainly, Jesus did not see it as boring.

I will confess that on the eve of my proposing to my then-girlfriend and now-wife, I did not spend the night in prayer. I was nervous and excited for the next day, but I did not ease my nerves through praying. Why not? I don't have a good answer. Surely marrying someone is a really important decision. I am going to spend the rest of my life with her, after all. But I didn't follow in Christ's example. I don't think I am the only one either.

## BUT WHY?

Why is this the case? Why do we not pray? Why do we find it to be boring? God is not boring. If anything, we are boring. God is the most interesting Being in the universe. He is literally keeping everything moving at this very moment. He is not boring; He is infinitely interesting. Yet, we find talking to Him to be taxing. What is the problem?

One of the most helpful books I have ever read on this subject is entitled *Praying the Bible* by Don Whitney.[1] It is a short, practical read that I would recommend you get and read. He asks the same question when he writes, "Indeed, why would people become bored when talking with God, especially when talking about that which is most important to them? Is it because we don't love God? Is it because, deep down, we really care nothing for the people or matters we pray about?" These are the questions we can often ask when we find ourselves bored with prayer. Is something wrong with me? Do I just not care? Do I just not love God? Whitney continues, "No. Rather, if this mind-wandering boredom describes your experience in prayer, I would argue that if you are indwelled by the Holy Spirit—if you are born again— then the problem is not you; it is your *method*."[2]

Let's have a group exhale. This is wonderful news! If the problem is not us, but rather our method, then we can be taught a new method. If we have been taught a terrible habit in our sport, then a good coach can correct it and help us improve. The problem is not that I cannot hit a golf ball, but rather a habit has been built that is holding me back. If the method changes, then things might just get better. I might be able to hit the ball straight after all. What is the method to helping improve our prayer life? Praying the Bible.

## PRAYING THE BIBLE

The Bible is God's Word given to us. It is God speaking directly to us through ink and paper. It is an amazing blessing we far too often take for granted. We know, and have discussed, how important it is that we spend time reading and studying the Bible. When we pray the Bible, we take the words of Scripture and turn them into prayers back to God. The monologue of Bible reading becomes a dialogue with prayer. Reading becomes a conversation.

Praying the Bible allows us to have a freshness in our prayer because each passage will be different from the previous. No two passages of Scripture are exactly same (except for a few identical chapters in Isaiah and Kings), even if they are similar, which means no two prayers of ours will be the same. One reason we often become bored is we repeat ourselves almost every time we pray. Just like how our conversation with our hero would get boring if we always said the same words, so prayer becomes boring when we have no variety. Praying the Bible helps to avoid monotony. We won't get bored by saying the same phrases on repeat. Though we can do this with any passage of Scripture, this method works particularly well with the Psalms.

The book of Psalms is the prayer book of the Bible. Throughout its pages we see the psalmist praising God, asking God for help, and longing for others to worship Him. They are prayers and songs that convey just about every emotion across the spectrum of our lives. We can get nervous praying to God when we are frustrated about something that happened to us. We might think a 'good Christian' would never speak to God in a frustrated tone. The psalmists disagree. Psalm 89:13-14 says, "But I, O Lord, cry to you; in the morning my prayer comes before you. O Lord, why do you cast my soul away? Why do you hide your face from me?" He is not shy about asking God where He is when he is in need. He feels abandoned by God because his friends have shunned him. Can you relate? Have you ever felt like this?

No matter how you are feeling, I can almost guarantee there is a psalm to go with it. Joy in God in victory; despair and sorrow; frustration and anger; heartbreak and pity. All of these emotions, and more, are found in this wonderful book. God has not forbidden us from taking our emotions to Him. He is not upset by our problems. Indeed, He calls us to cast our anxieties on Him because He cares for us (1 Pet. 5:7). The problem is we often don't know how to express our feelings toward God, and so we resort to saying the same phrases. Then, on top of this, we still feel guilty because we feel bored in prayer. It feels like a lose-lose situation. We are frustrated because we cannot express our feelings to God, so we quit trying. When we quit trying, we feel guilty. We need help.

Now that we know the Psalms are helpful in expressing our true feelings to God, it is time to learn the method. This method is simple: take the words of Scripture, and turn them into prayer. Whitney gives a great example when considering the 23rd Psalm. He takes the first line of Psalm 23, which says, "The Lord is my shepherd", and suggests we pray something like this, "Lord, I thank you that you *are* my shepherd. You're a good shepherd. You have shepherded me all my life. And, great Shepherd, please shepherd my family today: guard them from the ways of the world; guide them into the ways of God. Lead them not into temptation; deliver them from evil."[3] This is a genuine prayer that comes from a mind focused on a single verse of Scripture.

I don't want to speak for you, but I can speak for myself when I say this prayer is far more real, meaningful, and satisfying than many I have prayed in the past. Another example is from verse 3. It begins by saying, "He restores my soul." Whitney writes the prayer, "My Shepherd, I come to you so spiritually dry today. Please restore my soul; restore to me the joy of your salvation. And I pray you will restore to soul of that person from work/school/down the street with whom I'm hoping to share the gospel. Please restore his soul from darkness to light, from death to life."[4] He confesses his struggle to God through the promise that God restores our soul. This is a natural prayer when we feel dry in our walk with Christ. Psalm 23:3 just helps to bring it to expression.

We don't need to be shy with God on our struggles. If we feel spiritually dry, we can be open with Him. He already knows. Praying the Psalms provides the opportunity to give fresh words to our prayers and articulate them in a way that we might not be able to otherwise. We are taking the words God wrote and turning them into prayers in our own words. Whatever comes to our minds, as our eyes glance over the page, turn it into prayer. Something may seem unrelated but bring it to God in prayer. Using Scripture helps provide the guardrails we need to keep us on the road.

Remember, this isn't Bible study where we are trying to be laser-focused on discovering what the author means. We are allowing the Spirit of God to use the Word of God to stir our hears in prayer. Whitney writes, "So basically what you are doing is taking words that originated in the heart and mind of God and circulating them through your heart and mind back to God. By this means his words become the wings of your prayers."[5] There are no tests afterward for how well we understood the meaning. We are praying to God. We are having a conversation with our Creator and Savior.

It really is simple; and yes, it really does help. I am a man of routine. I don't like breaking a routine that I have established, even if it seems silly. For instance, my pastor jokes with me because I always go the backroad to church, rather than going an easier route. It is a little longer and takes a little more time. Why do I not go the easier route? It is because, when I was interviewing for the position, this was the way I went. I used it once or twice and have not changed since. I feel weird taking the other road.

When it comes to prayer, unfortunately, I can be the same way. I have my list of individuals that I want to pray for daily: family, friends, the church. This isn't wrong. It is a good and right desire to want to bring my family before the throne of God in prayer every day. However, it can become so stale and mechanical that I can catch myself wondering if I am even praying. Am I actually speaking to God, or am I just going through the list in my head?

Maybe you are like me. Maybe you get stuck, and you need some help. Praying the Bible is one simple way to improve your prayer life. It will allow for a variety in your prayers, even when the content has not always changed. I still pray for my family, friends, and church, but I am able to do it in a different way than just going through the list. Variety allows freshness to pervade, rather than staleness to rule.

## GODWARD PRAYERS

Along with this, another wonderful aspect of praying in this way is it enables our prayers to be far more God-centered. The goal of the Christian life is to know, love, obey, and glorify God. God is the point. The gospel of Jesus Christ reconciles us back to our Triune God through Christ's death and resurrection. Since we are to live for the glory of God in all things, which is what Paul means when he says, "whether you eat or drink, or whatever you do, do all to the glory of God" (1 Cor. 10:31), prayer is not excluded. Our prayers should be for the glory of God. Praying the Bible helps make this happen.

Why is this so? It is because we are human. We will naturally pray for the requests that are directly affecting us. Let's be honest. We are far more likely to pray for the test we have upcoming, or the doctor's appointment, or for a family member than we are for God to be glorified among the nations. Maybe you are more spiritual than I am, but I have been in and around churches for my entire life, and the prayers I hear tend to reflect the temporal rather than the eternal. We focus on what is right in front of us, what directly affects us. Praying the Scripture helps us in this fight for a Godward prayer life. It turns our attention back onto God, where it belongs.

How is this so? The Bible is a God-centered book. The Bible, from Genesis to Revelation, is a book about God. It is God's revelation to us. It is God telling us who He is and what He has done in the world. When we open to the Psalms, it is no different. The glory of God is on display in a myriad of ways. God is our Shepherd (Ps. 23); God is our rock, fortress, and deliverer (Ps. 18); God is merciful (Ps. 51); God reigns over all things (Ps. 97); God is our Creator (Ps. 104); glorious things of God are spoken in this wonderful book (Ps. 87); the blessed man is the one who delights in the law of God and meditates upon it (Ps. 1).

If we pray through the psalms, we will encounter the glory of God. If we pray using the words of the psalms, we will pray prayers that elevate God. We will pray in ways we may never have prayed before. Our eyes will be off of ourselves and put firmly on Him. We will magnify Him in a way that is fitting.

Pastor John Piper once wrote that there are two ways to magnify something, either like a microscope or a telescope.[6] To magnify with a microscope, you make something incredibly small look big. Think of your biology class looking at an amoeba through a microscope. You cannot see this organism with the naked eye. It is too small. When you use the microscope, you magnify it so that you can see what was always there. You take something small and make it big.

A telescope, on the other hand, is used for star gazing. When you go outside on a clear night and set up your telescope you are hoping to see more clearly something that looks really small. The difference is the star, moon, or planet are not small. They are massive. The issue is it is far away. The telescope magnifies it by allowing you to see what is big, but small when you look at it from earth. It takes something big and makes it visible.

We are to magnify the glory of God like a telescope, not like a microscope. The glory of God is far bigger than we can even begin to imagine. It is far greater than any planet you will ever see with even the most powerful of telescopes. When we magnify God, we are declaring Him to be as great as He actually is. We are not making our small God look bigger but are making our infinitely big God more visible. When we pray the psalms, we are able to see the glory of God in a closer way. Then, in response, we are able to praise Him as He should be praised. We are able to pray specifically, not generically.

Being specific is far better than being generic. I think we would all agree about this. I will give two examples. First, if I tell my wife that I think she looks pretty, then she will probably like it. If I tell her I love how her hair looks after she has spent time straightening it, or that I think her outfit is beautiful, and that it matches her eyes so well, she will probably be more pleased. When I am specific, she knows I paid attention. It means far more to her. Or take a critique from a coach at practice. If he tells you that you have been playing bad lately and walks away, that is not helpful. If he tells you that you have been rushing your shot on offense, without letting the play develop; or have been off balance on defense, which is why your opponent has been able to blow past you, it will probably be more beneficial to you. Those are details that enable you to adjust. You benefit from specifics.

God is glorious. God is powerful. God is wise. God is loving, kind, merciful, just, and gracious. What will help you most in your prayer is not generically spewing these out in a list, but rather seeing in the Bible examples of how God is merciful. See God's power on display as He brings Israel out of captivity in Egypt and praise Him because that same power works for your good (Ps. 105:27-36). Worship God as you confess your sin to Him through Psalm 51, and be blown away by His grace toward you. Cling to the specific promises when you have a need, not a broad one that may or may not apply. You will experience His presence more deeply as you use His words to speak back to Him.

## Practical Tips

Much like reading your Bible, a huge first step is having the desire to pray more. That is a great sign that God is working in your life. Whenever you have the desire to pray, make sure you do. God might be doing something through your prayer you may never know in this life. When I was in college, there was a day in which I felt the Lord pushing me to pray for a particular friend from high school. I had not spoken to him in over a year, but I felt the need to pray for him. I texted him randomly and said I was praying for him, and he responded that he had been struggling recently. He was very thankful for my prayer. If I would have ignored the urge, then I would have missed out on what God was doing.

The problem for me though, is not that I always feel the need to pray, but more often that I do not feel the desire to pray. What do I do when the desire is not there? We fall back on our commitment. We are still desperate for God even when we do not feel it. We are still dependent on God even when we feel in control. When life is going well, not a cloud in the sky, we need God. Therefore, we must commit ourselves to praying. As we saw earlier, if Jesus was committed to praying, then we certainly need to pray. Otherwise, we think we are stronger than our Lord. Pride can lead us to neglect prayer. That is a dangerous place to be.

I have found that pairing prayer with your Bible reading is a match made in heaven (quite literally, actually). Before you ever open your Bible, it is good to recognize our need for the Spirit to open our eyes that we might see what He wants us to see (Ps. 119:18). After all, the Holy Spirit is the Author of Scripture. If we can consult with the Author, then we would be foolish not to. As you sit at your desk with a closed Bible in front of you, pray. Only then should you open and read.

Pray during your Bible reading. Ask God to give you understanding when you come across something that doesn't make sense. I could not tell you how many times I ask God for help when I am studying a passage. How am I going to teach if I don't understand? I pray for help. I also pray for God to help me stay focused. I am easily distracted, and if I am still waking up, it can be rough. I pray that God will help me concentrate because without His help, my time will be wasted. Maybe you can relate.

Pray after you finish reading. Pray that God will help you to apply what you have read to your life. Pray that God will help you remember what you have read throughout the day. Pray for what you have going on during the day. Pray for your friends and family members. Pray that God would give you opportunities to share the gospel. Pray through a psalm or through the passage you have just finished. Try another method if you prefer (such as ACTS, which stands for adoration, confession, thanksgiving, and supplication).

If you struggle to pray for a long time, then set a timer. Be committed to praying for two minutes. It might be hard at first, but that is okay. Fight for those two minutes. Use your Bible as a guide to pray. When I say set a timer, I mean set a timer. Use your phone and don't move until the time is up. You just might find that, after a while, two minutes becomes easier and you are able to move to three minutes, five minutes, or ten minutes. Who knows what God will do in those few minutes of devoted time?

Pray with a group. Pray with your family or friends from church. Ask them to meet up to read the Bible and pray together. It might be a little awkward at first, but it just might become the thing you most look forward to in your week. Troubles eased, sins confessed, joys shared, and lessons learned might become a fixture of your week all the while we grow in our love for the Lord.

Use your down, in-between time for a better purpose.[7] You may not have thirty minutes straight throughout you day to stop and pray. What you might have is six, five-minute segments of time spread out over the course of your day. Two minutes here and there can add up over the course of a day. If you decided not to check your phone during those intervals, then you may pray for more than half an hour throughout the day without feeling the weight of having to pray all at once. Along with the time, it allows you to pray without ceasing, as Paul tells us to do (1 Thess. 5:17). Indeed, you will be closer to praying without ceasing by praying throughout the day than in one large chunk. Neither is wrong. Whatever works for your daily schedule is what matters. No one will judge you because you spend six five-minute sections praying to God, rather than one thirty-minute event. Don't be discouraged. Be committed to pray.

We need to spend time with our God, and it is a privilege that we get to spend time with Him. The fact that the God of the universe would listen to the prayers of sinners is staggering. Through Christ, we get to come before Him as sons and daughters. We cannot take that for granted. It is an amazing reality. Build prayer habits into your day, whether that is early, late, or throughout the day. Use the Bible to help focus your prayers on the One whom we are addressing. Commune with God. That is the goal. He is our goal in praying, our reason for praying, and power in praying. Enjoy your time with your wonderful, glorious God.

## Chapter Endnotes

[1] Donald S. Whitney, *Praying the Bible* (Wheaton, IL: Crossway, 2015).

[2] Ibid. 12

[3] Ibid. 29.

[4] Ibid. 31.

[5] Ibid. 32.

[6] John Piper, "How to Magnify God," Desiring God, June 30, 2022, https://www.desiringgod.org/articles/how-to-magnify-god.

[7] I first heard this from Chuck Lawless at a Southern Baptist Convention of Virginia meeting.

# Chapter 5:

# Worship

"Man, that church has great worship!" I loved the worship tonight! I could really feel God close to me." "I don't want to go to that place. The worship is terrible." If you were to hear these statements, what do you think these individuals would be talking about? If you have been around church for very long at all, you know exactly what they mean. They are talking about music.

I know I am not the only one who has heard the word 'worship' used in this way. However, the Bible means far more when it speaks about worship than merely music. If we are going to grow in spiritual disciplines and, more importantly, grow in our walk with Christ, then we must seek to worship Him as we were made to do. We were made to worship. The heart of sin is worshiping something other than God. Worship is a huge deal in Scripture. Anything less than right worship would bring less glory to God and less joy for ourselves. This is a trade we cannot be willing to make. We must open our eyes to worship as the Bible defines it, rather than as a playlist on our Spotify.

Before we tackle the question of what worship is, it may be helpful to think about what it isn't. That is where we will begin.

## What Worship Isn't

It might seem a little odd to begin by asking the question of what worship is not, but it will be helpful to untangle some of the ideas we have swimming around in our heads. First, worship is not music. Many of us equate worship with music. Worship can certainly include music, as we sing praises to our God. We are commanded to do so (Ps. 95:1; 96:1; Eph. 5:19; Col 3:16). However, that doesn't mean worship is music. It is so much more.

Take a ball, for instance. If I tell you to think of a ball, then something will come to mind. A football. A basketball. A tennis ball. Some type of ball comes to mind. However, just because you relate the word 'ball' to a soccer ball because you absolutely love to play soccer does not mean a ball is only a soccer ball. It includes it, but it is not only it.

What can happen when we equate worship with music is, as soon as we no longer like the music, then we think we cease to worship. If the right song isn't being played by the worship team then we cannot worship properly. Do you see how this can begin to center on us? Our preferences dictate whether God is worshiped or not. What God desires isn't on our radar. This is a problem, and it is one that is seen in the hearts and minds of Christians all around us.

I have witnessed church members leave because the music selection began to change. The commitment to the church was over. It was as if a breach of contract had taken place. The church failed to hold their end of the deal, namely to play the songs I like, so I feel no obligation to stay. They would no longer worship with us because the music was different. It is painful to watch, but it is all too common. When churches define worship as music, it builds into the minds of the people a subjective reality that does not fit with Scripture. Worship is not about our own music preferences, but about God's preferences.

Worship is not emotions. If you have ever been to church camp in the summer, then you have probably experienced some deep emotions in worship. They usually happen on Thursday night, the last night of camp. The preacher will preach a compelling sermon and the band will play as dozens of students rush forward with tears streaming down their faces. There are a lot of hugs and prayers to God in this night. It can be a powerful sight to see. I have been there, both as a student and as a leader.

Now, I want to make myself clear. I am not knocking this. God can use these moments and transform the lives of students. It was at a summer camp that God called me to ministry. There is nothing necessarily wrong with such moments. What I am afraid of, though, is students who leave this type of environment believing they can only truly worship God in those "big"moments. This is where I take issue. They cannot worship on Sunday morning in their home church because 'it just isn't the same'. This is a problem.

Emotions are important in the Christian life, but they are also dangerous. Fire can be helpful to cook your dinner, but, if it gets out of hand, you could burn your entire house down. Emotions can be the same. They are necessary to worship God. We are commanded to love the Lord with all of our heart, soul, mind, and strength (Mk. 12:30). We cannot do this without emotions. However, it is possible to have emotions and be wrong. Paul speaks of the Jewish people as having "zeal for God, but not according to knowledge" (Rom. 10:2). They were passionate for God, but they were dead wrong. We need more than just emotion.

Is God glorified when we are emotional, even sincerely emotional, but are off in our thinking? Matt Chandler gave the following example in a sermon. Say I came home from work and walked up to my wife, gave her a huge hug, looked her in the eye, and told her I loved her. I say, "I love you so much sweetheart! You are absolutely beautiful! I am not sure if it is your blonde hair or your blue eyes, but something about you tonight just makes my heart hurt with love." You might suspect that my wife is going to be flattered by all of this. She will be so happy that her husband cares so deeply about her. However, what I know, and you might not, is that if I said that to her, things would go really,

really badly for me. Why is that? My wife has brown hair and brown eyes.

Just having emotions, does not mean we are genuinely worshiping God. Just because we feel a warm feeling in our stomach does not mean we have trusted in Christ for salvation. Just because we are crying does not mean we are really repenting of our sins. Emotions may accompany these actions, but they do not equate to these actions. It is the same with worship.

When you worship the Lord, it will include emotions. It should include joy (Phil. 3:1; 1 Thess. 5:16), gratitude (1 Thess. 5:18), love (Jn. 13:35), as well as the other fruit of the Spirit (Gal. 5:22–23). However, having emotions and requiring a highly-charged scene to worship are not the same. We are to worship because of who God is not because of how we are feeling at any given moment. Otherwise, we are saying, "I have to be in the right mood to worship God. If I do not feel like it, then it won't be real. If it won't be real, then why should I bother anyway?"

Do you see how this again makes us the center of our worship? We become the one who determines when and how to worship. If I don't feel like it, then I am not going to do it. God will understand. This happens in churches all across the country. Christians wake up on Sunday morning and don't really feel like going to church, so they don't. The command of God to not neglect meeting together (Heb. 10:25) is set aside. We disobey God because we don't feel like worshiping God.

Our emotions and feelings are in flux. They change all the time, sometimes multiples times a day. Has this ever happened to you? You woke up feeling great. You had a great breakfast, mom packed your favorite lunch, and you are wearing brand new clothes to school. You look good and you feel good. Nothing is going to spoil your day. Until, that is, you accidentally spill coffee on your shirt on your way into school. Your brand-new shirt has a big stain on it, and your day is officially ruined. All of the happiness that you had walking out of the door is gone.

We cannot let our emotions define our worship because they change quickly. God is God and is worthy of worship, even when our feelings aren't strong. God's worth is never in flux. It is never determined by our situations. Even on our worst days, God deserves to be worshiped. Even on our best days, God deserves to be praised. Emotions will come and go, but God does not change. Worship is not emotions.

Finally, worship is not a service. I can certainly understand the confusion on this one. For the entirety of my life, in every church I have been a member, the Sunday service was called a worship service. There is nothing wrong with this. It signifies the focus of the service. We are there to worship. However, it can also be misleading. We can begin to think that worship does not take place outside of the 10:00-12:00 time slot on a Sunday morning. This is what the Lord gets every week. Anything that happens outside of that prescribed time is not worship.

We do worship during this time, but our worship is not to be restricted to the confines of this time, or the location of the church. As we will see, we do not need to be in a church building to worship. Indeed, most of our worship will be outside of the church walls. For all of the benefits of calling it a worship service, we must understand that worship itself is not restricted to a "worship service."

## What Worship Is

Now that we have discussed what worship is not, it is time to consider what worship is. The first truth we need to remember is God cares about how we worship. This should not even be a question in our minds. How we want to worship should not be on the radar. God decides how we are to worship. God is God, and we are not. His commands take priority over our preferences.

This is non-negotiable. One of the clearest ways this is demonstrated in the pages of Scripture is in the book of Exodus.

Think about the beginning of Exodus. Israel has left Egypt after God has performed ten plagues. These would have been gruesome to face. They are a clear display of the power of God. Even the seemingly less severe plagues would have been terrible. I love the summer. I would much rather the weather be hot than cold. I love being outside and enjoying the sunshine. One aspect of summer I do not like though, is the bugs, and especially the gnats. They are so annoying. No matter how hard you swat your hand over your head, they always come back. I think they can sense my frustration, and it fuels them on. To have the entire land covered in gnats and flies would have been miserable. This is what the Lord did. How much greater then, the death of the firstborn son (see Ex. 7–12 for full account)?

Israel obeyed God and left Egypt. They walked through the Red Sea on dry ground, while the Egyptian army was destroyed (Ex. 14). They were led by God and fed by God in the wilderness. Finally, they arrived at Mount Sinai where the covenant was established through the giving of the law, including the Ten Commandments (Ex. 20). One of the centerpieces of the worship of God for Israel was the ark of the covenant. This is where the Lord was to meet with His people (Ex. 25:22). It is a really important part of worship.

Since this was going to be the place where the Lord met with Israel, do you think He let Israel decide how it was going to look? Do you think God told them, like a toddler, "Make whatever you want, and I'll be happy"? Absolutely not. He gave them exact dimensions that they were to follow to the letter. He told them how big it was to be, how it was to be fashioned, what material to use, how it is to be moved, and what was to be on it (Ex. 25:10–22). Nothing was left to the whims of the people. They were to obey God. God made the decisions; the people were to do as they were told. Worship was too important to leave to sinful men to figure out. God spoke, and they were to follow.

God cares greatly about how we are to worship. Every sacrifice is meant to tell us how to worship. Thanksgiving, sin offerings, and cleansings are all a part of worship. Leviticus is Israel's manual for worship. God's concern for our worship has not changed since the coming of Jesus and the establishment of the church. There are non-negotiables for the worship of God. Some of these include: the preaching of the Word of God (Acts. 2:42; 6:4; 2 Tim. 4:2), prayer (Acts 2:42; 6:4; Col. 4:2; 1 Thess. 5:17), singing (Eph. 5:19), taking of the Lord's Supper (1 Cor. 11:17–34), and church discipline (Matt. 18:15–20; 1 Cor. 5). These should be present within the church at all times and in all places.

None of these should catch us by surprise. Indeed, we should be used to seeing many of them every week. Hearing the Word of God preached, singing praises to our King, praying to Him, and taking the Lord's Supper should be the regular outline for our church services. These are known as ordinary means of grace. God pours His grace upon us in the ordinary, common ways. They are un-spectacular to our eyes. Just because they are not an overt display of glory does not mean the glory and power of God are not present. He has commanded us to order our worship in these ways because this is how He has chosen to communicate His grace to us. He knows what is best for us. We are to follow.

There is nothing special in these events. God doesn't pour out His grace because we eat of the bread and drink of the cup. They aren't magic. What they are though, are exactly what we need. We need to hear the Bible preached so that we can hear directly from the Lord. Our deepest need is to hear from God. Our souls need to be fed through the Scripture. We were made to worship, and singing brings this to heartfelt expression, so we sing. We are desperate for God, for apart from Him, we can do nothing (Jn. 15:5), so we pray. The ordinances (baptism and the Lord's Supper) have been instituted by God as a picture of our new life in

Christ and to remind us of what was necessary for that new life. We will not grow as a Christian if we are not participating in these events. However, this is not ultimately what it means to worship. They are a part of worship, but not the totality of worship.

Worship is far deeper than simply being present and engaged when a sermon is being preached, music is playing, and the Supper is being distributed. Our whole lives are meant to be worship to God. There is nothing that is exempt from worship. This is far different from what we have often been told. It is far deeper, and much more meaningful.

Paul provides us with a helpful definition of worship in Romans 12:1–2. He writes, "I appeal to you therefore, brothers, by the mercies of God, to present your bodies as a living sacrifice, holy and acceptable to God, which is your spiritual worship." This text provides a helpful basis upon which we can see the Lord's definition of worship.

Simply put, worship is living for the glory of God in all aspects. Nothing falls outside of this scope. It is not based upon our own effort, but upon Him. This is crucial for us to understand. Your worship, and your life overall, is based upon the mercy of God that we have received in Christ. There is nothing that we have that we have not first received (1 Cor. 4:7). We worship God because of who He is and what He has done. The emphasis is on Him, and not on us. This is contrasting to the usual ways we define worship (the music we like and the feelings we have). It centers on Him.

Do you see what the sacrifice is that we are offering in worship? It is our own bodies. Everything we do, say, think, and feel is to be used in worship of God. Not only is everything meant to be worship, but this is also all the time. At no point, as a follower of Christ, is anything we do supposed to be understood as something outside of worship. This is important for us to understand.

Once we are a Christian, we are a Christian at all times. Since all of life is worship, all of life is to be worship.

What tends to happen is we view life in categories, or boxes. I have a box reserved for school, a box for sports, one for church, and one for family and friends. These boxes may overlap at times, like having friends at church. As a rule, though, they stay disconnected from one another. This means we often view worship as something that falls into the church box. It has nothing to do with my school box or my sports box. This leads us to acting one way around our family, another way at church, and a third way around our teammates in the locker room. The same person might not seem recognizable when you compare how he acts or talks in these different arenas. This is a problem.

When God saves us, He saves us to follow Him in all areas of our lives. There is nothing excluded from salvation, no part of us left out, and therefore, nothing should be excluded from our worship. There are no boxes that the Lord does not rightly claim. This is what it means for Christ to save to the uttermost in Hebrews 7:25. He saves completely. Nothing is left out. all of our boxes now go into the one box of Jesus. It all belongs to Him.

We are to present our bodies to Him, daily. We don't take any days off in our walk with Christ. There are no vacation days or trips away. Jesus tells us we are to pick up our cross daily and follow Him (Lk. 9:23). We are to do so as a living sacrifice, holy and acceptable. Our lives are to be lived in holiness, in obedience to God. Unlike the sacrifices listed in Leviticus, this one is living. We have already died with Christ and have been raised to walk in the newness of life (Rom. 6:4). Our lives belong to Him, and our worship is offering it back to Him in obedience every single day.

Practically, though, how does this look? What exactly does this mean? It seems pretty abstract on the surface. Paul has given us the answer in verse 2. He writes, "Do not be conformed to this world, but be transformed by the renewal of your mind, that by testing you may discern what is the will of God, what is good and acceptable and perfect." Our lives are not to be conformed to this world, but rather are to be transformed through the renewal of our minds. We are not to follow the world but are to follow Jesus.

The world around us wants to conform us to its own image. It is often not shy about this. If we are not careful, we will be greatly influenced by what our eyes see and our ears hear. You say phrases that you have never said in your life, but your favorite character on a show used it. Your attitude can become coarse and easily irritated based upon the music you hear.

I have seen it in my own life. There are shows that I cannot watch, not necessarily because there is something sinful (like nudity), but because of how it affects me. If the main character is snarky and rude, then I can catch myself doing the same. Music is the same way. There are songs I have not heard in years, and the moment they come on; I know every word. Culture has a way of sticking with you. It influences us and conforms us to itself, often without us ever realizing it.

John is clear when he writes, "Do not love the world or the things in the world. If anyone loves the world, the love of the Father is not in him" (1 Jn. 2:15). Being a part of the world and a part of the kingdom of God isn't an option. It is one or the other. You cannot have your cake and eat it too. The world wants your soul, and Christ died to save your soul. To choose the world is to be an idolator. To choose Christ is to worship as we were made to do.

We are not to be conformed to the world around but to be transformed to be more like Christ. This happens through the renewal of our minds. How do we have our minds renewed? It begins with what we feed our minds. The content that goes in will determine the content that comes out. We cannot expect garbage to go in and a masterpiece to pop out. It doesn't work like that. You may have heard your dad say to you, "you will get out of it what you put into it." There is a lot of wisdom in this. If we aren't willing to put forth effort for a sport or instrument, why would we expect to master it? How much more when it comes to our walk with Christ.

We cannot constantly feed our mind with sinful images and sounds and expect holiness to flourish. Yet, this is often what we do. Take something like pornography. It is not possible to engage in this and not have your mind warped by it. It will affect you. It may be subtle at first, but it will wreck your world. When it comes to the culture, we tend to watch and listen to the same things as everyone else. We binge-watch the same shows, even if they may be dishonoring to God. We blast in our cars the same music, even when the words convey a lifestyle contrary to God's design and often blaspheme God. We really don't look a lot different from our friends. Brothers and sisters, this isn't good.

What we need to fill our minds with are things that will help us focus on Jesus. Jesus is the One whom we desperately need, far more than catching up on our current Netflix show. Paul tells us, in 2 Corinthians 3:18, "And we all, with unveiled face, beholding the glory of the Lord, are being transformed into the same image from one degree of glory to another." When we behold the glory of the Lord we are transformed into the same image. We grow by looking. We are transformed by focusing on Christ. We will never be like Christ, nor reach the world, by conforming to the world. We need to be okay with missing out for the sake of something better.

It is usually at this moment that many will scream out 'Legalism!'. Anything that hints of rules will be quickly denounced as legalism. Legalism is real. It is when someone attempts to tie salvation to a certain moral act, rather than only repentance and faith in the finished work of Christ. Legalism is a dangerous reality of which we need to be aware. However, not being conformed to the world is not legalism. It is obeying Jesus. It is being conformed to the image of Christ.

No. We are not saved because we do not watch a show with nudity or listen to music with swearing. There are plenty of people who do neither and are still under the wrath of God as sinners. These things will not save us However, those who are saved will want to please their Lord by being conformed to Christ. We desire holiness because it brings glory to Jesus. We have found something we want more, so we gladly set aside the potentially sinful, or at least not helpful, for something that will enable us to love Jesus more deeply.

What we are talking about here is like the fruit of a tree, and not the root. The presence of apples on an apple tree does not make the tree alive. We know this because we can pull the apple off of the branch and eat it. The tree does not die as a result. The root system gives the tree life. If we uproot it, the tree will die. The apple simply shows the tree is alive. In the same way, conformity to Christ does not make one a Christian. However, conformity to Christ out of love is a good sign the individual is a Christian. Jesus tells us to look at the fruit of a person's life as evidence of salvation in Luke 6:43–44. I am not the first to make this connection. Jesus tells us the same.

We have our minds renewed by focusing on Christ. Anything that will help you in this process should become a normal part of your life. Reading your Bible is non-negotiable. We know Jesus in the pages of Scripture. We cannot do without the Bible. Does Christian music help you to focus on Jesus, then blast it in the car. Whatever will stir your affection for Jesus should be your pursuit. Do you like to read? Read something that will help you learn more about Jesus.

The flip side of this coin is also to be aware of what will cool your love for Jesus. A particular TV show may not be sinful, but it may not be helpful. The jokes in the show may make you laugh at something that makes Jesus weep. You may be able to watch it and still focus on Jesus, but you may not. You need to know your own heart and limitations. Do not put yourself in a situation that will dampen your walk with Christ. Eternity is far more important than the temporal. Jesus is more important than music and media. Are you okay to set aside a show for the sake of Jesus? Is that a question you are even willing to ask?

It is not wrong to have social media, for instance. It is a great way to stay connected to people that you know. However, if you spend your time comparing yourself to other people, feeling inferior because you are not as attractive, athletic, or smart, then it is not helping you love Jesus. If you live for the 'likes', then you are a slave to the opinions of others. This isn't the freedom that Christ purchased for us (Gal. 5:1). We aren't worshiping as we were made to do, as we are called to do. We have begun to worship something other than God. It has become an issue that must be addressed. Worship is too important to take chances on iffy content.

Our worship leads us to look more like Jesus. When we look more like Jesus, then we know the will of God for our lives. This is how Paul closes verse 2 of Romans 12. He writes, "that by testing you may discern what is the will of God, what is good and acceptable and perfect." When our heart's desire is to be more like Jesus, we will have no trouble knowing the will of God. This might sound odd because many of us have an overwhelming desire to know the will of God, and yet it seems so elusive.

God's will for our lives is far easier than we often believe. Paul tells us the will of God in 1 Thessalonians 4:3. He writes, "For this is the will of God, your sanctification". Our sanctification, our being made more like Jesus, our not being conformed to this world but being transformed by the renewal of our minds is the will of God for our lives. We make it far more complicated than it needs to be. We treat it like a pirate's treasure map of which we only have a small piece. We believe we can never know the will of God, and He's already told us!

God's will for your life is to have your whole life center on worshiping Him. Wherever you are, and at all times, this is His desire. From the huge decisions like college and relationships, to the small decisions of eating breakfast, we are to worship God. Or as Paul says, "whether you eat or drink, or whatever you do, do all to the glory of God" (1 Cor. 10:31). This is our spiritual worship. Whatever we do, even eating and drinking, is to be done for the glory of God, that we might be conformed to Christ, and live as living witnesses to the watching world. Jesus says it this way, "Let your light shine before others, so that they may see your good works and give glory to your Father who is in heaven" (Mt. 5:16).

This is how we are to worship God, not as an event or a feeling; not when the music hits just right and the band is killing it; we are to worship God in all of life. In Spirit and in truth (Jn. 4:24), through right belief and affections. The entire person is to worship. The sooner we understand this, the sooner we will live for Jesus fully and see Him glorified in all we do. This is our great aim in worship, the glory of Christ.

# Chapter 6:

## Service

When I was growing up, I absolutely loved Disney movies. I still do actually. As a 90's kid, I am convinced this decade is the high mark of Disney animation. One of my favorites was *Beauty and the Beast*. We had this on VHS (if you don't know what this is, it is how we watched movies before DVDs and online streaming services). I watched it all the time. I can still sing every word to most of the songs which will come in handy as my daughters get older.

One of the most well-known songs in this movie is entitled *Be Our Guest*. When Belle arrives and switches places with her father, who has been imprisoned for stealing a rose, she is sentenced to life at the castle with Beast. Unlike a normal prisoner, though, she is given a room. She initially refuses to go to dinner with the Beast, and so she is told that she is not to eat at all. However, the lovable servants have other plans.

When she comes down and asks for something to eat, they not only provide her with a banquet feast, but also a little entertainment. They sing this upbeat song about their longing to be of service. For too long, they have sat idly by, for the castle was now empty since the curse was placed upon them. Now that they have a guest, they are ready to begin serving again. They are prepared to do everything in their power to make the stay more comfortable for this scared young lady.

As a Christian, we have been saved, not so that we can live a comfortable life of ease until we get to heaven. We have been saved to serve others. Any walk with Christ will have service at its heart.

Our Savior came not to be served, but to serve (Mt. 20:28; Mk. 10:45), so why should we expect anything less?

It is a discipline that we must develop. It will not always come naturally. It will not always be easy. It may be awkward. It may not always be people that you like or who are easy to serve. They may be picky or rude. They may not appreciate your service. God may call you to serve someone who wants nothing but your harm. That is the case for a lot of Christians across the world. What drives this type of commitment to serve, even at our own expense? Why should we continue to serve even when we receive nothing in return? This is the focus of this chapter.

## CHRIST'S EXAMPLE

What was Jesus's mission? What did He come to do? How you answer that question will have a major effect on how you view the Christian life. We covered the gospel in a previous chapter, so we already have an idea of why Jesus came. He came to rescue us from the wrath of God by taking our place. He stood in our place condemned that we might go free through faith in Him. His resurrection from the grave proves the work has been finished (Jn. 19:30; Rom. 4:25). Our salvation and hope for eternal life rest solely in Him. This was the ultimate mission of Christ. This is what He came to do. However, throughout His ministry, He gives us little glimpses of purpose that we must see.

When I was in elementary school, the best, most important position a student could have was that of line-leader. Everyone wanted to be first. There is a heavy responsibility in leading the class to the library, cafeteria, and the playground. It wasn't for the faint-of-heart. Not everyone could handle it. Or, at least, that was what it seemed like to us kids. It never really dawned on us that everyone would be going to the exact same place with the difference being only a matter of seconds. We all wanted this coveted position.

Elementary school kids are not the only ones who want to be first. Seeking to be first in line was also the request of two of Jesus's disciples, James and John. They were a part of the Twelve. They had left everything to follow Jesus. They followed Jesus around, heard Him preach, had parables explained privately, and witnessed the miracles. They were even in the inner circle of Jesus, getting to witness the Transfiguration (Mt. 17:1–2). Only three disciples were there, and they were in the three.

They were in a prime position; and yet, they wanted more. They were not content to just arrive at the destination like everyone else. They wanted to be the line-leaders. They wanted to sit at His right and left hand (Mk. 10:37). They were not content to just be a part of the group, they wanted to be His go-to guys. They wanted to be second-in-command. That is a huge request. It was a bold request.

Like a lot of students in my elementary school, they were 'kissing up' to the Teacher. Plenty of students would go and ask the teacher if they could be the next line-leader. They wanted to know in advance, so that, when the time came, they would be ready to assume their place. As frustrating as this was for me and the rest of the class, I cannot imagine asking such a request of the Lord of the universe. The passage tells us that "When the ten heard it, they began to be indignant at James and John" (Mk. 10:41). The others were not happy with these two brothers trying to snake their way to the top. How Jesus responds would leave an indelible mark, not only on James and John, but also on the entire group. What would Jesus do? Would He grant their selfish request?

In reply, Jesus makes this statement, "For even the son of Man came not to be served but to serve, and to give his life as a ransom for many" (Mk. 10:45). Instead of fighting for a better position, James and John should be like Jesus and focus on serving. The attention is turned away from position and squarely onto service. What they did, and not their rank, should be their greatest concern.

There is so much wisdom in this reply. It is amazing. Instead of boldly rebuking them before everyone, He calls them to Him and reorients their hearts and minds. Instead of putting them on blast and making them an example, He teaches. Jesus is not like the rest of the world. Other leaders use their power to their own advantage. They want to rule and call the shots. History is filled with men and women who rise to power and never want to give it up. They want to make the decisions. A brief glance over the last hundred years of history displays this clearly in men like Adolf Hitler and Joseph Stalin. The consequences are usually horrible.

Jesus, on the other hand, is the Lord of all. He has every right to exercise His authority. He has every right to command the world to serve Him. Yet, He has come to serve others. His mission is not one of self-focus, but of self-sacrifice for the good of others. He was born in the manger not in a palace to rule in this life. He will rule, and is now ruling, but He saves through serving others through His death and resurrection. He is the Good Shepherd who lays down His life for the sheep (Jn. 10:11).

James and John needed to learn that prominence in the Kingdom of God does not look like being the one in charge, but rather as the one who serves. It does not look like status. It looks like sacrifice for the sake of others. This is a lesson that is often difficult to learn. Jesus though, was not content to simply teach a lesson with words. He was more than willing to step into the role of servant that all might see. He was going to make it clear that He has come to serve and not to be served. He makes this abundantly clear on the night of His arrest, in the upper room, with a towel and a bucket of water.

When you have only a limited amount of time with someone, you are far more intentional with how you spend those moments.

The final moments of a person's life are usually filled with words of love and forgiveness. A family member holding a grudge wants to make things right before the person passes away. Even something lighter like graduation from high school is filled with reminiscing of the good times spent together. There is a lot of emotion at the prospect of going your separate ways. We want these moments to count. We do not want to waste them.

On the final night of Jesus's life, when He knows He is about to be arrested, tried, suffer, and be crucified, we understand that Jesus would use His time perfectly. We would do well to pay attention to these final moments. As the clock is ticking, Jesus makes every second count. Everything Jesus does is intentional. However, we can also understand an added weightiness to His words in these final moments. John 13–17 provides an amazing look into this scene. It begins in a surprising way.

John adds an urgency to this scene as he begins chapter 13. He writes, "Now before the Feast of the Passover, when Jesus knew that his hour had come to depart out of this world to the Father, having loved his own who were in the world, he loved them to the end" (Jn 13:1). What a beautiful beginning. Jesus was not ignorant of what was before Him. His arrest did not catch Him by surprise. He knew what He was going to face that very night. Yet, He loved His own in the world to the very end. It was love that drove Him onward. It was love that led to His actions, both on the cross and in the upper room.

Have you ever questioned Christ's love for you? Have you ever sinned and thought, "that's it! Jesus is probably done with me?" I know I have. I have felt the bitter pain of wondering if I had out sinned the grace of God. Take heart. Remember these words. If you are in Christ, they are a wonderful promise for you too. Jesus loves His own in the world to the very end. Nothing will separate us from the love of God in Christ Jesus (Rom. 8:38–39). His love carries on. What a beautiful reminder as the scene opens.

John then tells us the devil had already put it into the heart of Judas to betray Jesus (Jn. 13:2). The final plan has been set in motion. They are in the endgame. Jesus, knowing this, "rose from supper. He laid aside his outer garments, and taking a towel, tied it around his waist. Then he poured water into a basin and began to wash the disciples' feet and to wipe them with the towel that was wrapped around him" (Jn. 13:4–5). Jesus washed His own disciples' feet. A job that is reserved for a slave is performed by the King.

I love going to the beach. It is my favorite vacation. I would rather be sitting on the beach with a book or playing in the ocean than be almost anywhere else. However, there is one part of the beach that I do not like: sandy feet. Don't get me wrong. I don't mind the sand on my feet when I am on the beach. It is when I am leaving the beach that makes it rough. It gets on your sandals. You have to spray them off, and you can never quite get it all, so you carry it with you. I understand why Anakin Skywalker doesn't like sand. It really does get everywhere.

Washing my feet after a day on the beach is gross. How much worse would it have been for Jesus to wash His disciples' feet? They walk everywhere. The road is dusty and dirty. The feet would have been the worst, most dirty part of their bodies; and yet, Jesus stooped down and washed their feet. He didn't have a hose to spray them off. He had a bowl of water and a towel around His waist. He would have been eye-level with their feet. The hands that formed humanity in the Garden washed the feet of His creation.

This was work for a servant, not for the leader. It was below the pay grade of anyone but a servant. No one wanted this job. On top of this, Jesus isn't a normal leader, He is the King of the universe. This should not have happened. Jesus should not have been the One who washed their feet. It was highly inappropriate. Yet, He is the One who willingly washed them. What is amazing, though, is that Judas was still present. Jesus washed the feet of the man who was about to betray Him; and He knew it.

Why would Jesus do this? Why would He willingly do something no one else wanted to do. Why would He take on such a lowly task? Why would He do what was so degrading as washing another man's feet. The good news is, we do not have to wonder. He tells us.

John 13:12–15 says, "Do you understand what I have done to you? You call me Teacher and Lord, and you are right, for so I am. If I then, your Lord and Teacher, have washed your feet, you also ought to wash one another's feet. For I have given you an example, that you also should do just as I have done to you."

If Jesus was willing to wash the disciples' feet, we ought to be willing to serve others, no matter how lowly or costly. This is the lesson. This is the example He has left for us. If our Lord and Teacher was willing to wash feet, then who are we to refuse any opportunity to serve others? We have no excuse. We have no reason to refuse. I'm sure James and John were stunned and cut to the heart when they heard the words and saw the actions of Jesus. They could see how selfish they really were.

Why should we be willing to serve other people? It is because Christ served. Not only did He serve in His death and resurrection, but He served in the small tasks as well. You might say you are willing to serve in laying down your life as a missionary in a foreign country, but are you willing to serve by washing the dishes at home or church? Are you willing to babysit so a young couple at your church can have a night out? Are you willing to pick up trash around the church, so the person who cuts the grass doesn't have to? Are you willing to hand out tracts and share the gospel to your friends at school? Are you willing to serve?

Our problem is we often want to serve in the spectacular, rather than the mundane. Washing dishes is boring. Why can't I serve on a short-term mission trip? You can! Why not both? If we put restrictions on when and where we are willing to serve, then our heart is not set on serving but on our own preferences. Christ gives an example of serving. This is what we are to follow. Small ways or big ways, we are to serve.

## PROPER MOTIVATION

Jesus left us an example that we are to serve. That is abundantly clear. What is our motivation to continue to serve when it gets hard? What happens when no one appreciates what we are doing? What happens when no one sees us as we work hard? What should keep us going? The answer is love.

One of the most beloved portions of Scripture is the parable of the Good Samaritan. I am willing to bet you have heard this at some point in your life. It is the story of the Samaritan man who was willing to help someone in need, even at great cost to himself. It did not matter that the man in need was of another ethnicity We are told to be like the Good Samaritan.

Do you remember the context of this parable? A lawyer approaches Jesus and asked a question, "Teacher, what shall I do to inherit eternal life?" (Lk. 10:25). This question makes sense on the surface. There is no more important question in the world than the question of salvation. Nothing matters more than inheriting eternal life. Maybe we give him a pass on the question, even though the religious leaders were notorious for trying to trap Jesus. Maybe this was a genuine question.

Jesus responds by asking him how he read the Law. The man responds well, quoting the two great commandments of loving the Lord with all one's heart, soul, mind, and strength, and loving one's neighbor as himself. Jesus commends the lawyer and tells him to obey, and he will live. So far so good, at least in theory. It is the execution that we lack.

What we must recognize, and the lawyer failed to, is our utter inability to keep these two commandments. The whole reason Jesus was standing before them was because no one is able to keep the Law and inherit eternal life. They could not perfectly obey. All have sinned and fall short of the glory of God (Rom. 3:23). Jesus had to come because the lawyer did not love God and his neighbor as he should, nor could he ever do so. Jesus had to bear our sin. He could not merit eternal life on his own, and neither can we. This man did not understand it.

What is worse is, not only did he not understand, but he was arrogant. How do we know this? Where most people would have wisely thanked Jesus for His advice, this man presses his case further. The conversation had gone well. He had received an answer. He should have moved on, but he didn't. He wanted more. Luke records, "But he, desiring to justify himself, said to Jesus, 'And who is my neighbor?'" (Lk. 10:29). This man wanted to justify himself before God. He wanted to know who his neighbor was, not so that he could be sure to help him, but because he wanted to restrict the list of people he had to help. He wanted to force Jesus to define "neighbor" for all to hear.

"Who are you talking about, Jesus? My friends? People who like me? Surely, you don't mean everyone. Whom must I help, and whom may I ignore?" These are the questions the lawyer is asking. He is not seeking a greater understanding but trying to get out of doing work. He wants to justify himself based on what he is already doing, rather than make sure he is obeying completely.

If you want an example, try telling a toddler to clean up his toys. The questions will start flying. Why should I clean them up? Which toys? May I keep some of them out? What if I am still playing with this one? I like that one and don't want to put it away. On and on the toddler goes. The lawyer wants to limit those for whom he is responsible. Jesus, however, turns the table completely. He isn't having it.

The parable of the Good Samaritan is meant to show us we are responsible to serve anyone who needs our help. The question is not 'who is my neighbor?' but 'am I a neighbor?'. Am I keeping the two commandments rightly by loving those around me? This is the essence of loving God and loving neighbor. We cannot love God if we do not love our neighbor. We are not loving our neighbor if we are neglecting their needs. If we love with words only, then we are not really loving at all.

So, what is the motivation to continue to serve? Love. We express that love in service to others. If we have experienced the love of God in Christ, then we must love others. Jesus tells us, in John 13:35, "By this all people will know that you are my disciples, if you have love for one another." If we do not have love for one another then we show the world that we do not belong to Jesus. We will be identified as Christians by our love. If we love one another, then we will serve. As James tells us, faith without works is dead (Jam. 2:17). To say you love your brother and not be willing to help when you have the resources to help is to show you don't actually love. Love leads to action.

Paul makes this clear in his letter to the Galatians. He writes, "For you were called to freedom, brothers. Only do not use your freedom as an opportunity for the flesh, but through love serve one another. For the whole law is fulfilled in one word: "You shall love your neighbor as yourself" (Gal. 5:13–14). Christians have been called to freedom in Christ. That is a glorious thought! We, of all the people in the world, are the ones who are truly free. We have been freed from the dominion of sin (Rom. 6:14), and the fear of death (Heb. 2:14–18).

How should we use this freedom? Is this a pass to do whatever we want? No. We have been freed so that, in love, we would serve one another. We have been freed to serve those in need.

In our lives, we are outward-focused, others-centered. This is the fulfillment of the first and second great commandments. Why have you been saved? You have been saved to serve others. Why are you to serve others? Because you love God with all you are and your neighbor as yourself. This is our motivation. This is true freedom and will stand out in a world focused only on itself. Surely this is what Jesus had in mind when He said, "Let your light shine before others, so that they may see your good works and give glory to your Father who is in heaven" (Matt. 5:16). We bring glory to God and get to know Him more deeply by serving others in love. Isn't this our great goal in the Christian life?

## BUT HOW?

The question I hope you are asking is this: where do I start? I pray you have a real desire to serve others because you see your Savior serving. I pray you will want to love others because God "showed his love for us in that while we were still sinners, Christ died for us" (Rom. 5:8). If this is how lavishly God loved and served us, even while we were His enemies, there should be nothing off limits in our service to others. We have no excuse to neglect the needs of others.

Jesus gives us a look into what the final judgment will look like in Matthew 25:31–46. We see the separation of every person into one of two groups: the righteous or the unrighteous. How Christ distinguishes these groups is by their deeds. Did their lives reflect genuine saving faith in Christ, or did it not? He speaks to the righteous, in verses 35–36, "For I was hungry, and you gave me food, I was thirsty, and you gave me drink, I was a stranger and you welcomed me, I was naked, and you clothed me, I was sick, and you visited me, I was in prison, and you came to me.'" Do you see how ordinary these deeds are? There is nothing spectacular here. They simply saw a need and served.

The righteous respond with a little confusion, wondering when they served Jesus in this way. They never saw Him in need and rushed to help. Jesus then tells them, "Truly, I say to you, as you did it to one of the least of these my brothers, you did it to me" (Mt. 25:40). In serving others, they were ultimately serving Jesus. They did not recognize it, but this is exactly what they were doing. When they helped someone in need, they were serving their King.

On the other side, the unrighteous are cast out, away from the presence of God. The reason? They failed to act in the way the righteous did. As Jesus says, "For I was hungry and you gave me no food, I was thirsty and you gave me no drink, I was a stranger and you did not welcome me, naked and you did not clothe me, sick and in prison and you did not visit me" (Mt. 25:42–43). When they protest by saying they never saw Him in need, Jesus responds in a similar way, "Truly, I say to you, as you did not do it to one of the least of these, you did not do it to me" (Mt. 25:45). The result is the righteous going into eternal life and the unrighteous into eternal punishment. We cannot say our service is unimportant in the Christian life.

The person who has been made a new creation in Christ Jesus will love and serve (2 Cor. 5:17). This parable does not teach that we earn our salvation by helping those around us. What it reminds us is a person who has been saved by grace through faith will lead a life of good works, which have been prepared by God for us to walk in (Eph. 2:8–10). A saved sinner will love in a brand-new way, in a way that reflects the love of God.

Where should you start? Think practical. What are the needs around you? Could you serve at the homeless shelter? Could you serve at a food bank? Could you cut grass for an elderly couple in your church? We don't need to make it more complicated than it needs to be. A huge blessing would be simply to ask your pastor what needs there are in the church. As a student pastor, I love hearing the question 'what can I do to help?'. Setting out food, stacking chairs, or staying after a few minutes to help clean may not seem like much, but they are huge acts of service in the life of the church. They aren't spectacular, but they are necessary.

We shouldn't wait until we are asked to serve. We need to be proactive in seeking ways to serve, not worrying about being seen or getting the credit. This is massively important. Our goal is serving the Lord, and not being seen by others. We don't need an audience. We don't need to post our service on Instagram so that others can see. When we do, Jesus tells us those likes will be our only reward (see Mt. 6:3–4 for an example).

Our heart should be focused on Christ. Paul says, "Whatever you do, work heartily, as for the Lord and not for men, knowing that from the Lord you will receive the inheritance as your reward. You are serving the Lord Christ" (Col. 3:23–24). Whatever it is that you do, work hard. Work hard because you are ultimately working for Christ. You may receive commendation and thanks, but that isn't your goal. We have been saved, so we serve.

Find a place to serve. Make a commitment to serve. It will not always be easy. There will be moments you may want to quit. Our service never depends on the response we receive. We serve because God has so loved us in Christ that we want to love others in response. Serving may be a gateway to a gospel conversation you may not have had otherwise.

Find something you are good at or like to do and see if you can use those gifts to serve others. However, just because you may not feel gifted in a certain area is not an excuse not to serve. No one needs a specific gift to vacuum a floor in the nursery at church. No one needs a gift to go to a nursing home and talk to some church members who are unable to go to church. It takes a willingness to go.

No matter what your task, never forget you are not alone. God is working in you and through you. Paul makes this clear when he says, "For this I toil, struggling with all his energy that he powerfully works within me" (Col. 1:29). God was working in Paul's working, giving him the energy to carry on. God will work in your working. Discipline yourself in serving others. Whether big or small, do it for the glory of God out of love for Christ and others (1 Cor. 10:31). Do it, and watch God work in and through you. You will experience more joy in Christ than you could imagine when you follow His example in serving others.

# CHAPTER 7:

## STEWARDSHIP AND GIVING

Imagine you were an alien. You were dropped into the United States of America for a week to learn our ways. This is a recon mission. In that single week, you watch our television shows, watch some of our movies, and listen to our music. You travel all across the country, from coast to coast, big cities to small towns. What do you think you would find to be the most important thing to Americans? I am willing to bet money would be near the top of your list.

As a culture, we love money. Everything centers on money. I am constantly blown away by how much money professional athletes make in a year. To play a game, they sign contracts sometimes in the hundreds of millions of dollars. Why? Do they really need that much? Is playing a game really that important? Will their lifestyles improve because they add millions to the millions already sitting in their accounts?

Money, in and of itself, is not evil. There is nothing wrong with making a good living, if one uses the money properly. Indeed, throughout the Old Testament, you will see individuals blessed by the Lord with incredible riches. A sign of the blessing was the material prosperity. Look at individuals like Abraham, Isaac, David, and Solomon. God blessed them with all the material they could ever want.

Think with me about one man in particular. Job was clearly blessed materially of the Lord. His wealth is hard to imagine. He had 7,000 sheep, 3,000 camels, 500 yoke of oxen, and 500 female donkeys, on top of a lot of servants. It is said this man was the greatest of all the people in the east (Job. 1:3). I have never lived on a ranch, but that seems like a lot of animals. In a day in which paper currency was non-existent, and bartering was the main way of doing business, this man had everything. And, Satan understands this. When he gets permission from the Lord to test Job, he says, "Does Job fear God for no reason? Have you not put a hedge around him and his house and all that he has, on every side? You have blessed the work of his hands, and his possessions have increased in the land" (Job. 1:9–10). It is clear the Lord is responsible for Job's prosperity. God blessed Job.

Do you remember what happens next? Satan, with permission from God, takes away Job's wealth, family, and finally his health. In the course of a few minutes, everything is gone. His entire life is flipped upside down. What will Job's reaction be? What would your reaction be? What would you do if your house caught fire and everything was lost? I know that is an awful scenario to think about, but try it. How would you react? Would your belief in God be shaken to its core? Would you no longer want to follow God since He allowed your possessions to go up in smoke? This was Job's real-life test. Would his possessions stand in between his relationship with God?

For Job, his reply was, "Naked I came from my mother's womb, and naked shall I return. The LORD gave, and the LORD has taken away; blessed be the name of the LORD" (Job. 1:21). Is this the right answer? Should he have had remorse over what he had lost? The text then says, "In all this Job did not sin or charge God with wrong" (Job. 1:22). Job's reply was correct. He did not charge God with wrong, even though he understood God was ultimately behind this in allowing Satan to take everything away from him. God could have stopped it, but He didn't. God was not wrong. God gives blessing as He sees fit and is allowed to take it away as He sees fit. It is all in His hands. He is God. Job learns that lesson the hard way.

By the end of the book, after Job has had an unhelpful discussion with some of his friends, the Lord speaks for Himself to Job, stating that He did not need to explain His actions (Job 38–41). Job could not understand the least of what God was doing in creation, why would Job understand when God moves in the world? It is arrogance on Job's part to think God owes him an explanation. The works of God are beyond our comprehension. Job confesses his sin and repents for doubting the goodness of God and seeking to establish his own innocence. He had spoken without truly knowing the Lord (Job. 42:1–6). The final lesson had been learned: knowing God in a deeper way is greater than an abundance of wealth.

What does this story have to do with giving? A lot! If we have a wrong view of possessions, we will have a poor understanding of how we are to use them. Job's example shows a correct view of our stuff. If everything in life, as our culture tells us, is centered on money, we will spend our lives trying to accumulate more so that we can spend it on toys that we don't ultimately need, trying to impress people we don't really know. How many Instagram accounts are full of people buying items they don't need so that they can get 'likes' from total strangers? Don't laugh, you might follow some of these people. You are impressed with their vacations, outfits, cars, and technology. You like their posts and want to see more. But, this is a dangerously wrong view of possessions. As Jesus says in Luke 12:15, we must "be on [our] guard against all covetousness, for one's life does not consist in the abundance of his possessions. True life is found not in possessions but in a Person—the Lord Jesus Christ.

But we continually face pressure to put our hope in the next possession. For example, technology is advancing at such lightning speed that it becomes obsolete fast. When I was a senior in high school, I got my first iPhone. It was an iPhone 4. It was so cool. I was one of the few students in my school who had one. It was a big deal. Now, Apple is on the iPhone 16 (I think). No one younger than me remembers the iPhone 4, except that it was necessary to get to 5, 6, 7, and on. The height of technology in my high school career is now a piece of junk that isn't good for anything. It is a paper weight. Eventually, every possession we have will be obsolete. It will be thrown away and forgotten. Jesus will never lose His relevance to our lives. Eventually, every possession we have will be obsolete, but Jesus will never go out of date.

If this is how the world continues to progress, why would possessions be our all-consuming passion? Why would the accumulation of the 'next great thing' consume our thoughts when something newer will inevitably follow? This is a wrong view of our stuff; and yet, I am willing to bet it is how most of us think. I certainly do not exclude myself from this, as if new toys (and now books) continue to draw my heart. What can we do to alleviate the pull the world's goods have on us? The answer is to have a right view of our stuff and how we should use it.

Here is the reality that we cannot forget. We are finite. We are mortal. Everything around us is too. There is not one shred of material possession you can take with you into eternity. All of the cars, houses, phones, gaming systems, new sports equipment, clothes, shoes will be left on earth when we move into eternity. Therefore, it is foolish to spend our lives for things that will not last. When we stand before God in judgment, He will not care if we had a big house or nice car. He will concern Himself with our sin and whether or not we have repented and believed in His Son. Therefore, we must keep eternity in view as we consider our possessions.

So, how should we view our possessions? To start, we need to realize nothing we own ultimately belongs to us. Paul reminds us in 1 Corinthians 4:7, "What do you have that you did not receive? If then you received it, why do you boast as if you did not receive it?" Everything we have we have received from God. Everything. Every single thing we own has come from God. Since this is the case, we need to actually treat our stuff like it belongs to God. If we do, it will change how we use our possessions. They are not ours. We are just taking care of them for a while.

The problem is, we do not naturally view our possessions as though they are God's. We treat them as if they are our own. Here is an example that might hit a little close to home. It would be like a teenager being given an iPhone for the first time. As a fifteen-year-old, he doesn't work, so he has no way to pay for it. Not only can he not pay for the actual device because they are really expensive, but his parents have to pay for the service too. The teenager says the phone is his, but it ultimately belongs to mom and dad, right? Don't they own it? After all, they pay for every part of it.

What happens when the grades start to slip at school because all his time is spent looking at the phone? So many fun games and YouTube videos to watch. How could anyone spend time studying? His parents will likely take the phone as a result. At least, they probably should. Is this fair? To us, we would probably say, "yes." They own the phone. They paid for it and continue to pay for it every month. They have every right to do with it as they see fit. To the student, he would probably see it as incredibly unfair. Why should his parents be able to take something that rightly belongs to him? They can't do that!

This is often how we view our possessions in relation to God. We don't want to give it up because we see it as our own. We went to school and worked a job to pay for the car and clothes. They belong to us. However, God is the Creator of all, and as such owns everything therein. Nothing exists that He does not own. It is His by right. We are just borrowing it. Anything we have, we have received as a gift from God. What we are to do with it should be a reflection of this reality.

Since God has given us everything we have, why does He care so much about how we use it? If someone gives you a birthday present, then I doubt they check-in on you regularly to see how you are using it. Once the gift has been given, we usually feel we are free to do with it as we see fit. However, the major difference, as we have seen, is that God still owns whatever He gives. We don't own it. We are stewards of it. A steward is someone put in charge of someone else's property to use for a good purpose on behalf of the owner. This is exactly what we are. Our task is to be good stewards of what the Lord has entrusted to our care.

This is what Jesus is teaching in the parable of the talents in Matthew 25:14–30. We are the servants who have been given talents to use to expand His kingdom while He is in heaven. To be a good and faithful servant is to work hard on His behalf and see an increase. To be lazy should not be an option. In fact, to be lazy and bear no fruit is to show that you don't actually belong to Jesus. How can we know this? The two servants who worked hard were rewarded by the master, while the lazy servant was cast into utter darkness (Mt. 25:21, 23, 30). We need to be good stewards of what the Lord has given to us.

## A DEEPER ISSUE

Far deeper than our being a good steward, which is important, how we use our possessions reveals a deeper issue: our heart. God does not care about our stuff because He needs our stuff. He owns everything, or as Psalm 50:12 puts it, "He owns the cattle on a thousand hills.". No, He doesn't need of our stuff. Instead, he cares about our possessions as they relate to our heart. How we handle our wealth reveals who we truly serve, whether the Lord or an idol.

In the Sermon on the Mount, Jesus provides insight into how we are to live in light of who He is. Because Christ is King, we are not to be angry (Mt. 5:21–26), be lustful (vv. 27– 30), be anxious (Mt. 6:25–34), and other topics. One important topic Jesus tackles is our treasures. He warns us to not lay up earthly treasures because they will ultimately fail us. The moth and rust will destroy it, and thieves can take it away (v. 19). He concludes this thought with a powerful statement. He says, in Matthew 6:21, "For where your treasure is, there your heart will be also." Whatever we value most, there will our heart be.

What do you treasure most? Is your treasure a sport? If so, you will put time, energy, and money into it. Is it your appearance? You will watch make-up tutorials and spend a lot of money on pursuing the right look. Is it Jesus? If so, then your whole life will be centered on knowing, loving, and serving Him. What we treasure may be the most important question we can ever ask ourselves. We cannot ignore it because the answer will impact all we do.

What does this have to do with money? Is it a stretch that I connect this passage to our money? After all, didn't I just list alternative treasures that we can have that are not our money? Yes, I did. However, Jesus makes it about money only a few verses later. He says, "No one can serve two masters, for either he will hate the one and love the other, or he will be devoted to the one and despise the other. You cannot serve God and money" (Mt. 6:24). The explicit connection our Lord makes is between serving God and money. What we treasure matters. It has massive implications for our lives.

Loving God and loving money are mutually exclusive. You have to choose one or the other. You cannot truly love God if you also love money. If you love money, then you will not be obedient to God. If you are a follower of Christ, and you want to grow in your walk with Him, then we cannot love money. Money, and the things it can buy, cannot become an end in-and-of-itself. Our heart must belong totally to God. They are mutually exclusive. You can have one or the other, but not both. You can only serve one. Which will it be?

A biblical example of this exclusive relationship can be seen in Jesus's interaction with the rich young ruler in Mark 10:17–31. You will recall this young wealthy man approached Jesus, asking

Him what he must do to inherit eternal life. When Jesus responds with keeping the commandments, the man quickly adds that He has kept these commandments from his youth. What was he missing?

Mark sets the scene, "And Jesus, looking at him, loved him, and said to him, 'You lack one thing: go, sell all that you have and give to the poor, and you will have treasure in heaven; and come, follow me'" (Mk. 10:21). Did you notice Jesus's attitude toward this man? He was not being spiteful, condescending toward him because he was rich. He wasn't jealous of his money and so he wanted to knock him down a little. He looked at him and loved him. It was love for the man that led to this command. Jesus understood that treasure in heaven, namely Himself, was infinitely more desirable than any earthly treasure. It would have been unloving to have told him anything else. He was offering the rich young ruler something far better.

Do you believe that? I know our reaction can be quick. Of course, we believe it. But do we really? Would you be comfortable, and even glad, to give up everything you own if you got Jesus in return? Would you give up your game system or sport or car or relationship with family because you want Jesus more? I hope the answer is yes. I just want us to ask and answer the question honestly.

How did the man respond? Mark writes, "Disheartened by the saying, he went away sorrowful, for he had great possessions" (v. 22). He was faced with the choice between Christ and his possessions, and he made his choice. He preferred his possessions over Christ. Unless something changed, he would not inherit eternal life. His heart was in his stuff, not in his God. He had not kept the commands as well as he thought. Jesus initially asked only about external commands of murder, adultery, stealing, and the like (v. 19). However, what Jesus intentionally chose to pass over was the command of having no other gods before the Lord (Ex. 20:3). This at the head of the Ten Commandments. In calling this man to give up his goods, Jesus showed him his heart. He had other gods before God. His possessions were his treasure. He was not willing to leave them behind, even if it cost him his soul. This is a sad choice that many people make.

You might rightly respond, "I thought you said money wasn't bad! Now are you going back on yourself?" Absolutely not. Money is not sinful. Do you remember Paul's words in 1 Timothy 6:10? He writes, "For the love of money is a root of all kinds of evils. It is through this craving that some have wandered away from the faith and pierced themselves with many pangs." It is not money that is the problem. It is the love of money that is sinful and leads to all kinds of evil. It was not sinful for the young man to be rich. It became sinful when he refused to give it up for Christ.

Money is not the enemy. It is not wrong to have it. However, it acts as an EKG for our hearts. It scans our hearts to let us know what is going on internally. Do we love money? Do we want it at all costs? Do we care more about what it can bring us than about the God who has given it? Do we want the pleasure and status more than God? All of these, and more, are questions that money can answer about our relationship with Christ. We cannot serve two masters. If we serve money, then we are not following Christ. If we are serving Christ, then our view of money, and our possessions, must be based on how He designed for us to use it. It is to be a tool for the building of the Kingdom of God. Nothing more, nothing less. To view it in any other way is to make it an idol.

## Now What?

How are Christians to use their resources? We are to be generous. We are to have an open hand towards others. Take a coin in your hand. Clinch that coin tightly in your fist. Now, have someone try to take it out of that fist? It is hard to do isn't it? This is how we often are with our stuff toward others. We hold on to it tightly and refuse to let it go. We are like the toddler screaming, "Mine!

Mine!" Christians are to live not with a clinched fist, but with an open hand. If you open your hand with the coin on your palm, you are able to give it to the person in need. We are to be generous, not greedy.

Paul illustrates this principle using an agricultural metaphor. If the farmer sows only a little seed, then he should not expect to have a massive harvest. If you only plant two tomato plants in your garden, then you shouldn't expect anything more than those two tomato plants to grow. It is pretty simple. What should the farmer do? He should sow abundantly. He should give himself every opportunity to prosper. So, it is with our money.

We are to be generous with our property, giving to others as the need arises. We are to do this out of a heart that loves God and loves our neighbor. It is to be a joy. This is a way we can serve others. Paul writes, "The point is this: whoever sows sparingly will also reap sparingly, and whoever sows bountifully will also reap bountifully. Each one must give as he has decided in his heart, not reluctantly or under compulsion, for God loves a cheerful giver" (2 Cor. 9:6–7). We are to be a cheerful giver. We are to be glad in our opportunity to give to others. When we are a cheerful giver, God takes delight in us. We are reflecting Him.

Paul continues, "And God is able to make all grace abound to you, so that having all sufficiency in all things at all times, you may abound in every good work" (v. 8). Far from taking something from you, God is able to make all grace abound to you when you are generous. We are able to do more with what we have because God is our Treasure. He is not trying to rob us. He is not taking away from us something we need. He is giving us the opportunity to have more of Him. That is loving!

It is like asking a child to give up his one Hershey Kiss because you are going to take him out for an ice cream sundae. The child receives far more than he gives up. It is a clear choice when he sees the options. You can have the small piece of chocolate. I am going for the huge bowl of chocolate.

Paul goes on, "You will be enriched in every way to be generous in every way, which through us will produce thanksgiving to God" (2 Cor. 9:11). God may enrich us for the purpose of being generous. He does not give to us so that we can hoard it up, like trying to build a bomb shelter in our basement with food for years. He blesses that we might give to others, that thanksgiving to God would be produced. When we bless others, we get to praise God for the opportunity to help, and the person gets to thank God for providing. God is praised in both instances. In this way, the Giver is recognized as God, and we rightly give Him thanks for what He has done. Is this not a reflection of the gospel? God always gives first.

Jesus, by right, was worthy of all honor and praise. He owned every house in the world, and yet He did not have a place to lay His head (Mt. 8:20). He emptied Himself by taking the form of a human, when He could have grasped onto the glory of equality with God (Phil. 2:6–7). He did this to the point of going to the cross (v. 8). When He was offered the kingdoms of the world if He would simply worship Satan, He refused because He knew His heart could only serve One (Mt. 4:7–11). Jesus chose love for God over love for money. He chose to be generous with His life, leaving us an example to follow (1 Pet. 2:21).

If Jesus was willing to be generous with His life, surely, we can be generous with our possessions. His life meant more than my stuff. We have no excuse for not being generous. After all, as a Christian, we are committed to following Christ. Anything less is playing a game. God owns it all. We are His stewards. Jesus was generous with far more than money. We are to be generous with our money. God loves cheerful givers. We are to be cheerful givers as a reflection of our treasure in Him. Our love for God means we give money its proper place.

When we have money in its proper place, we are able to be content or satisfied whether we have money or not. Hebrews 13:5 says, "Keep your life free from love of money, and be content with what you have, for he has said, "I will never leave you nor forsake you." Why should we seek to keep ourselves from the love of money? It is because we have Jesus. He promised to never leave us or abandon us. Isn't that far greater than anything money can offer? No price can be put on that.

Paul offers one other warning, from a passage already quoted in part, "But godliness with contentment is great gain, for we brought nothing into the world, and we cannot take anything out of the world. But if we have food and clothing, with these we will be content. But those who desire to be rich fall into temptation, into a snare, into many senseless and harmful desires that plunge people into ruin and destruction" (1 Tim. 6:6–9). The great gain of the Christian life is godliness with contentment. This is far greater than seeking after wealth. Why? It is because those who desire to be rich fall into temptation and can easily plunge into ruin and destruction. We could cite examples from our culture of individuals who have had it all — fame, wealth, power — and yet have committed suicide as a result. The temptation to become rich is real. It is alluring. It leads to destruction. Paul looks at the two and says he will take Christ. The gain is in godliness with contentment.

We are able to be content with plenty or hunger, abundance or need. Trusting that we can do all things through Christ who strengthens us (Phil. 4:10-13). It is our love for Christ that leads us to give. When we see our money and possessions in light of the gospel, we are able to be content and live generously. This will stand out in our watching world.

## WHERE TO START

As a student, you may never have thought about giving as a part of your commitment to the Lord. It may not have been on your radar. However, much like our worship, God cares about every aspect of our lives, and that would especially include one so important as our possessions. If it reveals our heart, then surely the Lord would care about it. Here is the encouragement I have for you: start giving early.

It will be easier to start when you are fifteen than wait until you are thirty. If you are willing to give to the Lord out of a weekly allowance, then it will be easier for you to give out of a paycheck. The amount is not as important as the heart behind it. The widow's penny commended by Jesus as more valuable than all the large sums given to the offering by the rich because "she out of her poverty has put in everything she had, all she had to live on" (Mk. 12:44). She was far more generous, and gave far more, than those who gave a far greater amount. The Lord cares about the heart.

What can you give that is generous? Is there something you can sell and give the proceeds away, something you no longer need or use? A tithe is a wonderful place to begin, but we want to be characterized by our generosity rather than a strict adherence to this Old Testament principle.

There are moments in Scripture where an extravagant gift is given, such as Zacchaeus giving away half his goods to the poor (Lk. 19:1–9). Jesus did not command him to do this but commented that "salvation has come to this house" as a result (Lk. 19:9). His heart was transformed by Christ, and this could be seen in how he handled his money.

Start early and set aside money every week, every other week, or even every month for the purpose of giving it away. My recommendation is to give it to the church (this will be discussed further in the next chapter). Don't let your age keep you from giving. Paul told Timothy, "Let no one despise you for your youth, but set the believers an example in speech in conduct, in love, in faith, in purity" (1 Tim. 4:12). Surely giving would be included in this. Set others an example by gladly giving, even when it looks small.

Seek to be consistent in your giving. This will be a discipline. It will be easier some weeks to give than others. At these moments, when the cost is felt, we look to Christ, remembering what He has done, remembering everything already belongs to Him, and we give.

Who knows what person you might encourage by your generosity? God may use your giving to draw people to Himself. After all, if you care so deeply about your walk with Christ that you are willing to give money to your church, then you might see others begin to take their relationship with Christ more seriously, or even unbelievers to consider Christ. The students around you in school and church may just take notice when you are willing to put your money where your mouth is. The Lord may use you in amazing ways, reaching people you may not even meet until eternity, all because you were disciplined in your giving.

Don't wait. Start giving generously. Don't worry about the amount. Give. Then keep giving. Christ gave more than we can repay, and that should drive us to give all the more.

# Chapter 8:

## In Community

Spiritual disciplines are habits we need to build into our lives. No matter the age, every single Christian is to grow more and more to be like Christ. The disciplines are necessary to live in faithfulness to Christ. They drive us to Christ, and we cannot live without Him (Jn. 15:5). The earlier they can be understood and applied, the better. I cannot tell you how thrilled I am that you care enough about them to read this book. It shows you have a real desire to mature as a believer.

These habits are just that, habits. They are disciplines for individuals. No one can read the Bible for you. Your parents cannot pray in your place. Sure, they can pray for you, but this will never replace your communion with God. Your pastor cannot give your money in the service of the kingdom (at least, not without a lawsuit following). As much as I long to help you, I cannot use these disciplines for anyone except myself. You need to develop them for yourself. However, just because they must be embraced by every individual Christian does not mean that we do them alone. We need one another. We need the church.

I want to finish this book with one final plea: be a part of a local church. You will not succeed in your walk with Christ, you will not grow as a Christian, and you will not worship properly without the church. You were made to be in a community. Christ died and rose again not just to save persons, but to create a people. We need one another.

God has saved us and placed us into His body. We are a part of the Bride of Christ. God cares deeply about His church. A body and a bride are beautiful pictures of how God views the church. We cannot obey Christ and disregard the church. It is not pleasing to God. There are plenty of Christians who say they love Jesus, but do not love the church. I am willing to bet you know people who say they are a Christian but rarely, if ever, darken the door of the church. They don't see the need. They don't see the church as necessary. It is just an add-on they don't feel they need to embrace. This does not honor God. It does not bring Him glory. It is disobedience. The church is a non-negotiable.

Say you and I spent a lot of time together and became close friends. We share a love for golf, so we play a round every week. We get to know each other as we play. You even come over and have dinner with my family, getting to know my wife and daughters. One day, on the golf course, you look at me and say, "Look man, I really like you. We have grown into great friends and I am thankful to God for you. I just have to tell you. I really don't like your wife." Do you think that is going to excite me? Do you think I am going to be understanding about this? Probably not. I would not feel honored by how much you like me if you do not like my wife. I love her more than I love you. Our friendship will end long before my marriage will.

If this is our natural response to a statement like this, how much more will God be dishonored if we seek to follow Him without the church? We would never be so bold as to speak that way to God. We would never dream of it. Yet, this is exactly what we do when we fail to prioritize church. When church isn't that important, this is the message we are sending to the God of the universe. We are telling Jesus, 'I love you, but I hate your bride'. How do you think He would react to this?

We are to love the church. We are to be committed to the church, not because it is perfect, but because Christ gave Himself up for it (Eph. 5:25). Each of these disciplines are personal, meaning you need to develop them in your own life. No one can do that for you. However, they are never meant to be private. You cannot make it on your own.

I am a huge nerd when it comes to the Marvel Cinematic Universe. I have loved these movies, especially the Avengers movies. One of the premises of the first Avengers is that each hero was strong alone, but none of them could face the threat posed by Loki on their own. Iron Man, Captain America, Thor, the Hulk, Hawkeye, and Black Widow had to team up in order to save the world (though it seemed like New York took an absolute beating during the fight). They were great on their own, but they were better together.

We need each other. We were not made to pursue Christ on our own. We were saved to be a part of the body. Each of these disciplines functions best when we are accountable to one another in the context of a local church. In this final chapter, we will go back over the six disciplines we have discussed and see them in their place in the church. The church is not and cannot be treated as optional for the Christian. We are commanded not to neglect meeting together but are to encourage one another and stir up one another to love and good works (Heb. 10:24–25). This happens in the church.

## BIBLE STUDY

How should the church help us in our Bible study? There are a few ways. The first is in how we are to study the Bible. When we hear the Scripture preached and taught faithfully and clearly, we are also learning how we are to read our Bibles. In my own ministry, I try my best to show the students where I am getting my points in the text of Scripture. I want them to not only see what I see, but also to see how I saw them. It is as the old saying goes, if you give a man a fish you feed him for a day, but if you teach him to fish, you feed him for a lifetime.

When you come to church, pay attention to the sermon. Pay attention to how the pastor is handling the text. Where is he getting his main points? How does he connect his points? How is he paying attention to the details? All of these are important and will teach you how to read your Bible. I have learned more about how to read my Bible by hearing sermons than I have in a classroom. Come ready to listen and learn.

Along with this, ask your friends to read the Bible together. This will keep you accountable for actually reading your Bible. You will also learn from one another about what stood out in the text. You will learn a great deal from your friends as you are reading it together. Commit to reading the Bible through in a year with a leader and some friends. This will be both challenging and beneficial as you learn more about God through His Word. As Proverbs 27:17 tells us, "Iron sharpens iron, and one man sharpens another."

We are meant to help one another. No one can read the Bible for you. You have to pick it up and open it. I cannot do it for you. Your parents cannot do it for you. Your student pastor cannot do it for you. That doesn't mean you have to do it alone. They can help you by reading it with you. Don't miss out on what the Lord is teaching you through His Word by neglecting the people He has placed around you in the church.

## EVANGELISM

As I mentioned in the chapter on evangelism, this is one discipline in which I struggle. I am an introvert that is content to be left alone to my books. Outside of preaching and teaching, I get nervous meeting new people and talking to them. If left to myself, I will not share the gospel with those around me. I know myself enough to know it will not happen. That cannot be okay with me. You might be in the same boat. You might be uncomfortable talking to people you do not know.

Maybe you are the opposite. Maybe talking to other people comes naturally to you. Praise God. Share the gospel with as many people as you have opportunity. Here is how you can help people like me. Share your stories. Tell others how the Lord is using you in sharing the gospel. It will encourage others, even the timid, to share. Having examples makes a world of difference.

Go out in groups to share the gospel at your local mall. Invite your student pastor to a Bible study with your friends at your school before class. Ask your pastor for resources to help. Ask questions that you may have heard from your lost friends that you couldn't answer. The more people who are involved in your evangelism the more likely you will press on in the work of sharing Jesus with others. Spend time praying for each other. Pray for the individuals with whom you are sharing by name. Invite them to your church, and introduce them to others.

In our evangelism, we can never forget the church. God did not save us to be alone. We were saved to be a part of the church. Any person who hears the gospel and responds in faith and repentance needs to be directed to a church. They need to join in with a local body so that they can be baptized and partake of the Lord's Supper. These happen in a church. They need to learn and worship and serve and give. They need the church. We will not grow without it. Don't forget about the Bride of Christ in your evangelism.

## PRAYER

Prayer is personal. We pray silently and out loud when we are alone. Prayer is our speaking to our Heavenly Father. However, we are also to pray together. Throughout the book of Acts, we see the church spending time in prayer together. It was central to their lives. There is no church without prayer. In our churches, we should be praying.

You might be thinking the last sentence is a little redundant. It is unnecessary because anyone who steps foot in a church for a service will probably hear a prayer at some point. Yes, we pray corporately, but are we praying as the pastor prays? Are we joining our 'Amen' of agreement when the pastor finishes? Or are we nodding off and wishing he would pray faster (doesn't he know how hungry we are)?

We need the church for our prayer. Much like evangelism, prayer can often get put on the back burner if we do not have a pressing need. We miss out on precious moments with Christ as a result. When we come together, we should spend time praying. When others pray, or speak about their prayer times, we are often encouraged in our own praying. Before Bible study at church, pray. Before a church event, pray. Before the worship service begins, pray. We will never look back at time in prayer and see it as wasted. Even if there isn't a group prayer, pray to yourself so that you can be prepared for whatever is to follow.

The church needs our prayers. Pray for your pastors. One of the biggest encouragements for a pastor to hear is when people say they are praying for him. I know this is incredibly meaningful for me. That someone would take the time and go before the Lord of Glory on my behalf is astounding and humbling. Your pastor is bearing far more than you will ever realize. He is dealing with people who are sick, in sin, in need, in marriage crisis, and who do not believe in Christ, and that and more in any given week. Pray for him. He needs it.

Pray for the other leaders in your church. Pray for fellow students. Pray for them by name. Ask to see the church directory, and pray for families. Pray for the service. Pray that God would open the eyes and hearts of the congregation to what He is going to say through His Word. We are to be characterized as a praying church. James tells us that we do not have because we do not ask (Jam. 4:2). Why not ask God to move in profound ways in your church? These are prayers that the Lord will hear.

## <u>Worship</u>

Worship should be something we do together. As we saw, it is much deeper than a service. Our entire lives are to be lived in worship to God. There is no part of our lives that falls outside of the command to worship. How will we mature in our walk with Christ and live as we have been called to do? We will do this through the support of the local church. The church is a collection of Christians who are pursuing the same goal, the glory of Christ. We are to stir one another up to love and good deeds, and that happens through our meeting together (Heb. 10:24–25). We need one another. Sanctification is a group project.

The book of Revelation is an intimidating book. It is full of imagery that is hard to understand. I know I do not understand a lot of it. However, there is one scene that is easy to understand and very moving. In Revelation 7:9–10, we read, "After this I looked, and behold, a great multitude that no one could number, from every nation, from all tribes and peoples and languages, standing before the throne and before the Lamb, clothed in white robes, with palm branches in their hands and crying out with a loud voice, "Salvation belongs to our God who sits on the throne, and to the Lamb!" This is the picture of worship in heaven. Before the throne of God, Christians from every nation and culture were worshiping the One true and living God. Can you imagine what this is going to be like? Every follower of Christ will be a part. We get to be a small part of it now in our local church.

When we come together to sing praises to God, hear the Word of God preached, pray together, take the Lord's Supper, give, and serve, we are anticipating heaven. We are living out on earth in a small way what eternity will be like. We need to be a part of this. For the good of our souls, we must find a community of believers in a local church to commit ourselves to. This is not optional. We need each other to help us worship.

We need accountability in our fight against sin. We need prayer as we start a new school year. We need wisdom to how to navigate a tough decision. All of these arenas are a part of our worship to God. Other Christians help us to worship more faithfully. Online church is not the same as gathering together. We need to be together every week to help one another on our way to heaven. Do not neglect your local church. You need them, and they need you.

## SERVICE

We can accomplish far more together than we can apart. A good team will beat a great player. One ant cannot gather much, but a lot of ants can gather more than we can imagine. Our small jobs, put together, will make a huge impact. The discipline of service works best in the context of a local church.

How can we know what needs are around us? Where can we begin? A good place to start is by asking our pastors or other ministry leaders. Are there any areas in the church that need volunteers? This is an easy entrance point. It doesn't take a lot of skill to play with young kids, but it does take a willingness to serve. As a parent of young children, I can tell you how big a blessing the nursery and children's workers are in a church. We would not be able to grow as believers without them.

Start small. Volunteering to be a smiling face at the welcome table at your church is incredibly important for the guests who arrive on Sunday morning knowing no one but looking for hope. Ask your student pastor about doing work in the community as a group. This will be a great opportunity to serve the area around the church, and it is also a lot of fun. Picking up trash in a park might not seem like fun, but if you do it with your friends from church it just might turn out to be a great day. Hanging door hangers about an upcoming event might lead to someone coming to Christ.

You could host a fall festival at your church. If I tried to paint a child's face, then the tiger would turn into an orange and black mess. Praise the Lord, because we are serving together, I don't have to paint. The more you can do together, the better. You will encourage one another, help each other.

There will be opportunities all around you if you are willing to look. Big or small, every job matters. Don't neglect the overlooked, underappreciated needs. God sees your service, even if no one else does. The kingdom advances as the people of God serve for the glory of Christ. Find your group at church and find a way to serve.

## GIVING

Much like service, more can be done together than on our own. It is no different with our money. The church is the place where we are able to sow for the Kingdom of God, giving to something that will benefit in eternity. Therefore, the church is to be the place where we give our money to the Lord.

The Lord has given you a wonderful gift in a pastor, or team of pastors, to help shepherd and teach you. Just as we will not grow apart from the community, the Lord has given us in His church, so we all bear the responsibility of giving to ensure the church is able to continue. Paul says, "Let the elders who rule well be considered worthy of double honor, especially those who labor in preaching and teaching. For the Scripture says, "You shall not muzzle an ox when it treads out the grain," and, "The laborer deserves his wages"" (1 Tim. 5:17–18). Pastors are to be given double honor, and those committed to the task of preaching and teaching are worthy of compensation from the church. This enables the pastor to study and preach to the best of his ability, thereby enabling the church to be properly fed the Word of God. It is to your own benefit to give.

Along with pastors, the resources need to heat and cool the church, equipment for the musicians, toys for the toddlers, and functioning bathrooms all require money. Ministry to the community and the nations are included when you give. Tracts to give your neighbor and services and events to invite them to require funding. When you give to the church, you are not just paying your pastor, you are joining in the mission and ministry of the church. You are a part of something much bigger than yourself.

I will not lay down a hard rule of how much we are to give. That is not my place. Throughout the Old Testament, we see a principle of the tithe, or ten percent given to God from the start of the harvest. There is good wisdom in this. However, what you see throughout the New Testament the principle of generosity. The tithe is not mentioned in regard to the church, though it is still helpful. However, since Christ gave His all, we should not settle for less. Has the Lord blessed you? Give more than ten percent in thankfulness to Him. Are you just beginning to give? Then start slow with the intention of building up as you go. Whatever is generous, maybe even a little stretching, should be our goal in our giving.

Don't wait to give. Our goal is a heart that loves the Lord such that we would willingly give whatever necessary to have Him. He is our ultimate Treasure. The world needs to see our heart belongs to Christ.

## CONCLUSION

Spiritual disciplines are crucial for the Christian life. We cannot expect to grow without them. Following Christ is hard, and we are told to count the cost (Lk. 14:25–33). Some of these might come easier than others, but we must seek to improve in them all. Trust me, it takes time, and even then, we will never be perfect. Don't let that discourage you. If anything, let it help you press on because the God whom we are seeking is more than worth it.

Praise the Lord that we do not have to do this alone. My prayer for you is that the Lord will bless you in your desire to follow Him in these ordinary tasks. There is nothing spectacular about them. Reading your Bible, praying, sharing the gospel, worshiping, serving, and giving are not flashy. They are not brand new and cool. They are the tools the Lord has given us for maturation. Brick by brick we are building the house of our lives. We are building in honor of the Lord, for His glory and the good of others. The new heavens and the new earth is our goal where we will spend an eternity with our Blessed Lord. Spend your time and resources investing in what will last.

The work will be hard. You can count on that. You will face opposition. Jesus warned us of this (Jn. 16:33). You are not alone. The Lord has given you the church to help you endure to the end, encouraging you, sharpening you, calling you to repent and trust Christ. We need each other. Finally, we are not alone because Christ has promised to never leave or forsake us (Heb. 13:5). Because Christ is risen and is with us, fight for these disciplines in your life.

I am so thankful you have shown the desire to obey Christ by reading this book. This tells me you are serious about wanting to pursue Him more. What a beautiful reality. He is more than worth any and all effort. We will find Him to be faithful through it all, wise beyond measure, beautiful beyond belief, gentle and lowly to the weary soul, and always good, loving, and righteous. This is our God. May He bless you in your walk with Him.

# APPENDIX:
## <u>GODLY LEARNING</u>

One final note that I think might be helpful, though one that is not explicitly found in Scripture, which is why I have placed it as an appendix and not a chapter. I wanted to make clear throughout the course of this book that we are to obey what the Bible tells us to do. This is why I have sought to show you from the Bible not just the 'how', but the 'why'. Without the why, the how is irrelevant.

There is one more recommendation I have, and that is to pursue God through reading. I know reading is not at the top of many of your to-do lists. However, it has proven invaluable in my life. I have grown so much over the years from reading people so much smarter than me. We are not the first group of Christians in the world. There is almost two thousand years of church history filled with Christians thinking deeply about the Bible, culture, and hard questions. It would be wise to tap into this deep well. Many of the deepest questions you may be asking have likely been asked by others before you. This wisdom is available in ways that would have been unimaginable even fifty years ago. The internet has opened all of history to you. A lot of it is even free!

Throughout this book, I have tried not to cite a lot of sources for one main reason: The Bible is the authority in our lives. Therefore, it is far more important to make my case from Scripture than from another author. I appreciate it greatly when other authors do exactly this. Indeed, it is why I am drawn to certain authors.

Paul tells us in Romans 12:2, "Do not be conformed to this world, but be transformed by the renewal of your mind, that by testing you may discern what is the will of God, what is good and acceptable and perfect." We are not to be conformed to this world. We are to be distinct from it. How are we to avoid conformation and be transformed? It is by the renewing of our minds. What you think about will drive what you do. Therefore, it is imperative that we fill our minds with what will help us love Jesus and live in obedience to Him. This is covered at length in the chapters on Bible study. However, we can renew our minds in reading outside of the Bible too.

Bible reading should always be the primary means of communing with God. He has given us His Word so that we can know Him. We can never neglect this and think we will grow. However, we can also recognize the benefits of reading others as well. These books will never carry the same authority as the Bible, but they can help us understand the Bible in a deeper way. Therefore, it is advantageous for us to read.

I will recommend a few different categories that have proven helpful for me. Feel free to read all of them, or none of them. These are just authors that the Lord has used to stir my affection for Jesus.

The first recommendation is Christian biographies. As a pastor, I want to do my best to shepherd the students entrusted to me as well as I can. However, I know I will make a lot of mistakes over the course of my life and ministry. Biographies allow me to step into another's shoes, to learn from their thinking, preaching, pastoring, and life both what to do and what not to do. A good Christian biography will teach Bible, theology, and practice. I recommend biographies on Charles Spurgeon, C. S. Lewis, Martin Luther, Dietrich Bonhoeffer as potential starting places. Their stories are really interesting for a lot of different reasons. If I can learn from mistakes of others, I can avoid making them myself. A critical mistake could be avoided by seeing what happened when another made it.

Read theology. I know that sounds terrifying, but it isn't as bad as many assume. I would love for students to pick up Calvin's *Institutes of the Christian Religion,* but I know it probably won't happen. We can be easily intimidated by the sheer size of the book. However, if you commit yourself to reading 3-5 pages a day, over the course of a year, you will read far more than you realize. Ask your pastor for a solid recommendation. Theology is seeking to know God. It is the most practical course of study you could ever take. Everything connects to God. Theology helps us make these connections well.

One of the easiest places to begin reading theology is to read your church's statement of faith. What is the doctrinal confession for your church? I have found these to be incredibly helpful because it articulates the core Christian beliefs in a short space. As a Southern Baptist, our statement of faith is the *Baptist Faith and Message 2000.* If you want to know what we believe, that is the best place to start. Reading your church's doctrinal confession will go a long way in helping you understand the Christian faith.

Find some authors who help you love Jesus, and dive headlong into them. For me, that person is John Piper. He has shaped my thinking on the Bible more than almost anyone I have encountered. I read and re-read much of his material. When I see he has a new book, it is preordered on Amazon. I could list a lot of people, but some recommendations are Piper, Albert Mohler, R. C. Sproul, J. I. Packer. I have also found Dane Ortlund's *Gentle and Lowly* and *Deeper* to be incredibly helpful. Again, ask your pastor for the authors who help fix his eyes on Jesus.

Because I am also a church history nerd, I cannot stop before recommending some Puritan works. I have been helped more by this group of Christians from England in the 1600's than almost any other group. It may sound weird, but it is true. If you have never read John Bunyan's *The Pilgrim's Progress*, please do. It is the story of the Christian life told as a journey to the Celestial City. It is so helpful. I have read it multiple times. For battling sin in your life, read John Owen's *Mortification of Sin*. It will help you in your battle against your flesh. These are just two that may help get you started.

Certainly, more could be added. We could fill another book on this topic. However, I just wanted to whet your appetite a bit and help to get your eyes off of yourself. We need to focus on our Triune God, His glory, and His work in the world. Godly learning will only help us in this pursuit.

# Works Cited

Packer, J. I. *Concise Theology*. Wheaton, IL: Crossway, 2020.

Packer, J. I. *Evangelism and the Sovereignty of God*. Downers Grove, IL: IVP Books, 2012.

Piper, John. "How to Magnify God." Desiring God, June 30, 2022. https://www.desiringgod.org/articles/how-to-magnify-god.

Piper, John. *Providence*. Wheaton, IL: Crossway, 2020.

"Plenary Definition & Meaning." Dictionary.com. Dictionary.com. Accessed September 21, 2022. https://www.dictionary.com/browse/plenary.

Smethurst, Matt. *Before You Open Your Bible: Nine Heart Postures for Approaching God's Word*. Leyland, England: 10 Publishing, 2019.

Sproul, R. C. *The Holiness of God*. Wheaton, IL: Tyndale House Publishers, 1998.

Whitney, Donald S. *Praying the Bible*. Wheaton, IL: Crossway, 2015.

# College&Clayton
### Press

ATHENS, GEORGIA

We are a publishing company dedicated to producing quality works in Christian history, theology, and biblical studies. Our goal is to help foster the love of God with the mind. We hope that such an endeavor will also lead to the love of neighbor. Our conviction is that the fruits of solid research and interpretation are more open, thoughtful, and generous individuals. Please visit our website for our upcoming titles and other articles explaining more about who we are.

**COLLEGEANDCLAYTON.COM**

HISTORY // THEOLOGY // BIBLE STUDY

# Also Available from
## College&Clayton Press

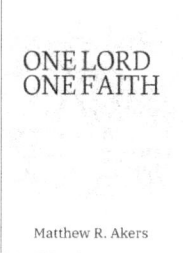

In *One Lord One Faith: Lessons on Racial Reconciliation from the New Testament Church*, Matthew Akers explores the deep racial divides that threatened the early church. Believers, who learned how to celebrate their unity by applying Christ's teachings to their lives, ultimately tore down the ethnocultural barriers that separated them. Their oneness astounded a world that had never seen this level of reconciliation. As a result of their commitment to love God and to love others, the Holy Spirit blessed their faithfulness, which convinced many that Jesus is Lord. The purpose of this book is to help twenty-first century American churches implement in their congregations the first century church's approach to racial reconciliation.

In *Bethlehem's Redeemer: Seeing Jesus in Ruth*, Daniel J. Palmer creates a Bible study for small groups or individual study that emphasizes the Messianic and salvific content contained in Ruth. Within the introduction Daniel offers a practical, theologically-minded hermeneutic for his readers to trace and emulate his method as he deploys it through the text of Ruth.

The Great Commission is both a climactic promise and triumphant command of the victorious King to His subjects. As such, it is a mandate to follow for all churches as well as all individual Christians. However, the Great Commission is not a standalone proof text or isolated command. It is rooted within a grand biblical narrative that extends from its beginnings in Eden to its consummation in the New Heavens and New Earth. In *The King's Command*, Josh Howard explores the all-encompassing scope of the Great Commission and it's claim on our lives as Christians.

In *Worship of the Triune God: Finding Delight in a Life of Worship*, Nathan Skipper sets out to show that the whole of the Christian life is an act of worship. Skipper does this by exploring the major themes of systematic theology through a doxological lens, rooting our understanding of God, salvation, the church, and the age to come in this chief end—"to glorify God and enjoy him forever." Skipper's project finds its core in the Book of Ephesians, which is itself a letter of high praise to the Lord. The reader is left understanding that Christian worship is more than just a weekly act. Worship is the reason for which we exist and the only way to find true purpose and delight.